Bloom's BioCritiques

Maya Angelou
Jane Austen
The Brontë Sisters
Lord Byron
Geoffrey Chaucer
Anton Chekhov
Stephen Crane
Emily Dickinson
William Faulkner
F. Scott Fitzgerald
Robert Frost
Ernest Hemingway
Langston Hughes
Stephen King
Arthur Miller
Toni Morrison
Edgar Allan Poe
J. D. Salinger
William Shakespeare
John Steinbeck
Mark Twain
Alice Walker
Walt Whitman
Tennessee Williams

Bloom's BioCritiques

GEOFFREY CHAUCER

Edited and with an introduction by
Harold Bloom
Sterling Professor of the Humanities
Yale University

CHELSEA HOUSE
PUBLISHERS
A Haights Cross Communications Company
Philadelphia

©2003 by Chelsea House Publishers, a subsidiary of
Haights Cross Communications.

A Haights Cross Communications ✈ Company

Introduction © 2003 by Harold Bloom.

Printed and bound in the United States of America

10 9 8 7 6 5 4 3 2 1

Library of Congress Cataloging-in-Publication Data

Geoffrey Chaucer / edited and with an introduction by Harold Bloom ;
Bonita M. Cox, contributing editor.
    p. cm. — (Bloom's biocritiques)
Includes bibliographical references and index.
  ISBN 0-7910-6181-7 (acid-free paper)
 1. Chaucer, Geoffrey, d. 1400—Juvenile literature. 2. Poets,
English—Middle English, 1100-1500—Biography—Juvenile literature. I.
Bloom, Harold. II. Series.
  PR1905 .G46 2002
  821'.1—dc21

                                        2002008449

Chelsea House Publishers
1974 Sproul Road, Suite 400
Broomall, PA 19008-0914

http://www.chelseahouse.com

Contributing editor: Bonita M. Cox

Cover Image © Michael Nicholson/CORBIS

Cover Design by Keith Trego

Layout by EJB Publishing Services

CONTENTS

User's Guide

These volumes are designed to introduce the reader to the life and work of the world's literary masters. Each volume begins with Harold Bloom's essay "The Work in the Writer" and a volume-specific introduction also written by Professor Bloom. Following these unique introductions is an engaging biography that discusses the major life events and important literary accomplishments of the author under consideration.

Furthermore, each volume includes an original critique that not only traces the themes, symbols, and ideas apparent in the author's works, but strives to put those works into a cultural and historical perspective. In addition to the original critique is a brief selection of significant critical essays previously published on the author and his or her works followed by a concise and informative chronology of the writer's life. Finally, each volume concludes with a bibliography of the writer's works, a list of additional readings, and an index of important themes and ideas.

HAROLD BLOOM

The Work in the Writer

Literary biography found its masterpiece in James Boswell's *Life of Samuel Johnson*. Boswell, when he treated Johnson's writings, implicitly commented upon Johnson as found in his work, even as in the great critic's life. Modern instances of literary biography, such as Richard Ellmann's lives of W. B. Yeats, James Joyce, and Oscar Wilde, essentially follow in Boswell's pattern.

That the writer somehow is in the work, we need not doubt, though with William Shakespeare, writer-of-writers, we almost always need to rely upon pure surmise. The exquisite rancidities of the Problem Plays or Dark Comedies seem to express an extraordinary estrangement of Shakespeare from himself. When we read or attend *Troilus and Cressida* and *Measure for Measure*, we may be startled by particular speeches of Ulysses in the first play, or of Vincentio in the second. These speeches, of Ulysses upon hierarchy or upon time, or of Duke Vincentio upon death, are too strong either for their contexts or for the characters of their speakers. The same phenomenon occurs with Parolles, the military impostor of *All's Well That Ends Well*. Utterly disgraced, he nevertheless affirms: "Simply the thing I am/Shall make me live."

In Shakespeare, more even than in his peers, Dante and Cervantes, meaning always starts itself again through excess or overflow. The strongest of Shakespeare's creatures—Falstaff, Hamlet, Iago, Lear, Cleopatra—have an exuberance that is fiercer than their plays can contain. If Ben Jonson was at all correct in his complaint that "Shakespeare wanted art," it could have been only in a sense that he may not have intended. Where do the personalities of Falstaff or Hamlet touch a limit? What was it in Shakespeare that made the two parts of *Henry IV* and *Hamlet* into "plays unlimited"? Neither Falstaff nor Hamlet will be stopped: their wit, their beautiful, laughing speech, their intensity of being—all these are virtually infinite.

In what ways do Falstaff and Hamlet manifest the writer in the work? Evidently, we can never know, or know enough to answer with any authority. But what would happen if we reversed the question, and asked: How did the work form the writer, Shakespeare?

Of Shakespeare's inwardness, his biography tells us nothing. And yet, to an astonishing extent, Shakespeare created our inwardness. At the least, we can speculate that Shakespeare so lived his life as to conceal the depths of his nature, particularly as he rather prematurely aged. We do not have Shakespeare on Shakespeare, as any good reader of the Sonnets comes to realize: they do not constitute a key that unlocks his heart. No sequence of sonnets could be less confessional or more powerfully detached from the poet's self.

The German poet and universal genius, Goethe, affords a superb contrast to Shakespeare. Of Goethe's life, we know more than everything; I wonder sometimes if we know as much about Napoleon or Freud or any other human being who ever has lived, as we know about Goethe. Everywhere, we can find Goethe in his work, so much so that Goethe seems to crowd the writing out, just as Byron and Oscar Wilde seem to usurp their own literary accomplishments. Goethe, cunning beyond measure, nevertheless invested a rival exuberance in his greatest works that could match his personal charisma. The sublime outrageousness of the Second Part of *Faust*, or of the greater lyric and meditative poems, form a Counter-Sublime to Goethe's own daemonic intensity.

Goethe was fascinated by the daemonic in himself; we can doubt that Shakespeare had any such interests. Evidently, Shakespeare abandoned his acting career just before he composed *Measure for Measure* and *Othello*. I surmise that the egregious interventions by Vincentio and Iago displace the actor's energies into a new kind of mischief-making, a fresh opening to a subtler playwriting-within-the-play.

But what had opened Shakespeare to this new awareness? The answer is the work in the writer, *Hamlet* in Shakespeare. One can go further: it was not so much the play, *Hamlet*, as the character Hamlet, who changed Shakespeare's art forever.

Hamlet's personality is so large and varied that it rivals Goethe's own. Ironically Goethe's Faust, his Hamlet, has no personality at all, and is as colorless as Shakespeare himself seems to have chosen to be. Yet nothing could be more colorful than the Second Part of *Faust*, which is peopled by an astonishing array of monsters, grotesque devils, and classical ghosts.

A contrast between Shakespeare and Goethe demonstrates that in each—but in very different ways—we can better find the work in the person, than we can discover that banal entity, the person in the work. Goethe to many of his contemporaries, seemed to be a mortal god. Shakespeare, so far as we know, seemed an affable, rather ordinary fellow, who aged early and became somewhat withdrawn. Yet Faust, though Mephistopheles battles for his soul, is hardly worth the trouble unless you take him as an idea and not as a person. Hamlet is nearly every-idea-in-one, but he is precisely a personality and a person.

Would Hamlet be so astonishingly persuasive if his father's ghost did not haunt him? Falstaff is more alive than Prince Hal, who says that the devil haunts him in the shape of an old fat man. Three years before composing the final *Hamlet*, Shakespeare invented Falstaff, who then never ceased to haunt his creator. Falstaff and Hamlet may be said to best represent the work in the writer, because their influence upon Shakespeare was prodigious. W.H. Auden accurately observed that Falstaff possesses infinite energy: never tired, never bored, and absolutely both witty and happy until Hal's rejection destroys him. Hamlet too has infinite energy, but in him it is more curse than blessing.

Falstaff and Hamlet can be said to occupy the roles in Shakespeare's invented world that Sancho Panza and Don Quixote possess in Cervantes's. Shakespeare's plays from 1610 on (starting with *Twelfth Night*) are thus analogous to the Second Part of Cervantes's epic novel. Sancho and the Don overtly jostle Cervantes for authorship in the Second Part, even as Cervantes battles against the impostor who has pirated a continuation of his work. As a dramatist, Shakespeare manifests the work in the writer more indirectly. Falstaff's prose genius is revived in the scapegoating of Malvolio by Maria and Sir Toby Belch, while Falstaff's darker insights are developed by Feste's melancholic wit. Hamlet's intellectual resourcefulness, already deadly, becomes poisonous in Iago and in Edmund. Yet we have not crossed into the deeper abysses of the work in the writer in later Shakespeare.

No fictive character, before or since, is Falstaff's equal in self-trust. Sir John, whose delight in himself is contagious, has total confidence both in his self-awareness and in the resources of his language. Hamlet, whose self is as strong, and whose language is as copious, nevertheless distrusts both the self and language. Later Shakespeare is, as it were, much under the influence both of Falstaff and of Hamlet, but they tug him in opposite directions. Shakespeare's own copiousness of language is well-nigh incredible: a vocabulary in excess of twenty-one thousand words, almost eighteen hundred of which he coined himself. And of his word-hoard, nearly half are used only once each, as though the perfect setting for each had been found, and need not be repeated. Love for language and faith in language are Falstaffian attributes. Hamlet will darken both that love and that faith in Shakespeare, and perhaps the Sonnets can best be read as Falstaff and Hamlet counterpointing against one another.

Can we surmise how aware Shakespeare was of Falstaff and Hamlet, once they had played themselves into existence? *Henry IV, Part I* appeared in six quarto editions during Shakespeare's lifetime; *Hamlet* possibly had four. Falstaff and Hamlet were played again and again at the Globe, but Shakespeare knew also that they were being read, and he must have had contact with some of those readers. What would it have been like to discuss Falstaff or Hamlet with one of their early readers (presumably also part of their audience at the Globe), if you were the creator of such demiurges? The question would seem nonsensical to most Shakespeare scholars, but then these days they tend to be either ideologues or moldy figs. How can we recover the uncanniness of Falstaff and of Hamlet, when they now have become so familiar?

A writer's influence upon himself is an unexplored problem in criticism, but such an influence is never free from anxieties. The biocritical problem (which this series attempts to explore) can be divided into two areas, difficult to disengage fully. Accomplished works affect the author's life, and also affect her subsequent writings. It is simpler for me to surmise the effect of *Mrs. Dalloway* and *To the Lighthouse* upon Woolf's late *Between the Acts*, than it is to relate Clarissa Dalloway's suicide and Lily Briscoe's capable endurance in art to the tragic death and complex life of Virginia Woolf.

There are writers whose lives were so vivid that they seem sometimes to obscure the literary achievement: Byron, Wilde, Malraux, Hemingway. But most major Western writers do not live that exuberantly, and the greatest of all, Shakespeare, sometimes appears to have adopted the personal mask of colorlessness. And yet there are heroes of literature who struggled titanically with their own eras—Tolstoy, Milton, Victor Hugo—who nevertheless matter more for their works than their lives.

There are great figures—Emily Dickinson, Wallace Stevens, Willa Cather—who seem to have had so little of the full intensity of life when compared to the vitality of their work, that we might almost speak of the work in the work, rather than even of the work in a person. Emily Brontë might well be the extreme instance of such a visionary, surpassing William Blake in that one regard.

I conclude this general introduction to a series of literary bio-critiques by stating a tentative formula or principle for gauging the many ways in which the work influences the person and her subsequent, later work. Our influence upon ourselves is always related to the Shakespearean invention of self-overhearing, which I have written about in several other contexts. Life, as well as poetry and prose, is overheard rather than simply heard. The writer listens to herself as though she were somebody else, and the will to change begins to operate. The forces that live in us include the prior work we have done, and the dreams and waking visions that evade our dismissals.

HAROLD BLOOM

Introduction

Chaucer—as Donald Howard eloquently showed us—led almost too interesting an outer life: fighting in two wars, endless travels in Europe, personal dealings with the kings and leading nobles of his time, and literary relations with most writers of note. Shakespeare, the only English writer who surpassed Chaucer, fought no wars, was never out of England, and for the most part confined his relations with people of power carefully to the theatrical sphere. It is not that Shakespeare's world was void of violence, but Shakespeare evaded angry events as best he could. We have comprehensive legal records concerning him, and they are virtually all commercial. There is nothing like the somewhat sensational document in which one Cecily Champain released Chaucer from legal actions concerning her rape: Chaucer doubtless had disbursed a large cash settlement.

In the 1380s, when Chaucer was in his prime, Richard II struggled desperately for power, and England was in turmoil. During the decade 1389-99, Richard gradually lost ascendancy, while Chaucer remained his faithful servant. Though the deposing of Richard by Henry IV possibly cost Chaucer nothing in patronage, it must have saddened him. In any case, a year later the great poet died.

There is a curious difference, almost a gap, between what we know of Chaucer's life and era, and his poetry. The age was violent, but Chaucer was an ironist of genius, and *The Canterbury Tales* and *Troilus and Criseyde* transcend their historical context. G.K. Chesterton remarked that Chaucer's irony was so large that sometimes we have trouble even seeing it. Chaucer is sublimely sly, whether in expressing his own pathos, or in acknowledging his authentic literary precursors, Dante and Boccaccio. Boccaccio particularly made Chaucer possible, in some of the same ways that Chaucer enabled Shakespeare to people a world. Chaucer's tales are *about* tale-telling, because Boccaccio had perfected the kind of fiction that is aware of itself as fiction. Stories rhetorically conscious that they *are* rhetoric behave very differently from stories that mask such consciousness. Clearly, Chaucer's heightened sense of story has some relation, however evasive, to the *Decameron*.

Chaucer likes to cite imaginary authorities, while avoiding any mention of Boccaccio, but that returns us to Chaucerian irony. Unlike Boccaccio, Chaucer will not admit to his own passional misadventures, except as jests, or as self-parodies. We are made confidants by Dante, Petrarch, and Boccaccio: Chaucer's anguish stays well within him. Part of Chaucer's genius emerges as self-distancing and comic perspectivism, anticipations of Shakespearean irony. What is extraordinary in Chaucer's own invention is his sense of personality, which allows the Wife of Bath, the Pardoner, even the Prioress (whom I just do not like!) each to speak in her or his own voice. The miracle of mature Shakespeare, which is the individualization of voice in Falstaff, Hamlet, Iago, Cleopatra and their peers, relies upon Chaucer's provocation to Shakespeare's developing genius. Sir John Falstaff is the Wife of Bath's son, as it were, and Iago's superb nihilism is anticipated by the Pardoner's joy in his own power of manipulation.

E. Talbot Donaldson, shrewdest of modern Chaucerians, illuminated Chaucer's two principal *personae*, Chaucer the Pilgrim in *The Canterbury Tales* and the narrator of *Troilus and Criseyde*. Chaucer the Pilgrim is everyone's favorite: friendly, more than tolerant, exuberantly receptive to every colorful scoundrel with whom he travels, but also always prepared to admire authentic goodness. The speaker of *Troilus and Criseyde*, presented as a would-be but unlucky lover, falls so intensely in love with Criseyde that most of us (men anyway) come to love her as

Chaucer evidently does. Chaucer the Pilgrim is the greater ironist; the narrator of *Troilus and Criseyde* is finally so heartbroken that he transcends his own ironies.

ELLYN SANNA

Biography of Geoffrey Chaucer

A Journey to Italy

Geoffrey Chaucer experienced his first major diplomatic assignment as a member of a commission sent to negotiate with the Duke, citizens, and merchants of Genoa, Italy. The commission was to choose an English port in which the Genoese might establish a business. Aside from the smattering of Italian that he had picked up as a child growing up in London—where his parents had done business with "pepperers," merchants who dealt with the pepper, then an exotic fruit—Chaucer's knowledge of the language at the time was limited to his own interactions with Italian merchants. When he set off for Genoa, then, he was able to communicate, albeit inelegantly, in Italian; by the time of his return, he would read Italian fluently. Furthermore, the Italian poetry to which his travels exposed him would become a principal influence on, and an integral part of, his writing.

Chaucer was paid 100 marks in advance for his work with the commission. He would ultimately be out of England for about a year, and on his return he would be paid another 138 marks as a reimbursement for his expenses. The total was considerable by fourteenth-century standards, and, more importantly, such a healthy payment indicates that the King valued Chaucer's service.

Genoa was warm and, to an Englishman even so well-traveled as Chaucer, certainly exotic. London in the fourteenth century was built mostly of wood, with slim, tortuous streets, and the mentality in the city was generally pragmatic. Genoa's ancient Roman streets were broad and smooth, its stone buildings tall and domed, and its people hot-blooded and full of song.

Chaucer loved music. He loved to study the structure of buildings and cities. And he loved observing different types of people. He was deeply impressed by Genoa. Everything about the city—the architecture, the art, the literature, and the music—left an impression on him, and all of it would radically alter his view of the world. Indeed, it was in Italy that Chaucer first discovered the poetry of Dante, whose *Divina Commedia* inspired Chaucer throughout his own career as a writer. Dante wrote of a love that transcended sensual pleasure and became a reflection on, or a reflection *of*, the divine. While his own attitude towards romance may have been more level-headed than Dante's, Chaucer was impressed.

It is also in Italy that Chaucer met the great Italian poet Petrarch, who, along with his young and talented follower Boccaccio, spent much of his time wandering through Italy and France in search of wisdom. Together Petrarch and Boccaccio sought out libraries, where they studied ancient Latin literature; they purchased old parchments and poured over them for new sorts of knowledge. They were equally fascinated by human nature, studying people as much as they did books and collecting stories full of particularly human detail. Petrarch's influence on Chaucer is clear; Chaucer began to follow the same pattern in his own life. Not only did he collect books and study ancient writers, but he too became a careful observer of human behavior—all of which would later appear in his work.

Chaucer's journey to Italy did not only influence his writing; it brought him the increased favor of the King. Within three months of his return from Italy, the King sent Chaucer to escort an Italian ship, arrested at the English port of Dartmouth, back to its master in Genoa. How Chaucer felt about the return is impossible to say, but clearly Chaucer was no stranger to sights other than those of his native England.

His voyages were long and dangerous, but as a result of his successful completion of the King's service Chaucer had secured a life of prominence and comfort. Through much of his life, loyalty would win him favor—various annuities, a large house, prestigious positions in government, and, most importantly, time to write.

CHAUCER AND THE FOURTEENTH CENTURY

Geoffrey Chaucer was born somewhere in England between 1340 and 1345. His father, John Chaucer, was a wealthy vintner in London and a master at his craft—a prosperous middle-class businessman who augmented his income by playing landlord to several houses in London. His wife, Agnes Copton, was wealthy in her own right.

Geoffrey's father's parents also were successful vintners—respected enough that his grandfather was appointed as deputy to the King's butler and served as a collector of the King's custom taxes, positions of no small prestige. Still, the family seems not to have been entirely stable in its prosperity: John Chaucer's aunt once kidnapped him in a plot to gain control of family wealth by marrying him to his own cousin. Her plans were foiled when John's soon-to-be stepfather and stepbrother stole him back. Despite such dramatic early turmoil, though, John Chaucer became a hardworking and equally prosperous adult. His reputation as a master vintner was well enough established to secure him a place in an expedition to Flanders with England's King Edward III (r. 1327–1377). Chaucer's exact duties on this trip are uncertain; he may have served as a wine authority, entrusted with providing drink for the King's household. In any case, his traveling with the King signals a certain favor and influence.

In 1349, when Geoffrey Chaucer was six or seven years old, his father gave up his offices to the King in order to manage some new property in the country that he had inherited through his wife. The Chaucers' move to the country may have saved young Geoffrey's life. In that same year, his grandfather, his uncle, his great-uncle, and a cousin all died of the Black Death. The immediate family was safely removed from London's infested streets.

London in Chaucer's day was a small, walled town with a population of about 40,000 people. The streets were often covered in waste, and the air likely smelled of wood smoke, horse manure, and garbage. Sanitary conditions permitted the "Black Death," a strain of the bubonic plague, to sweep the city regularly. Too, England itself was an unsettled place in the fourteenth century. The end of the Middle Ages brought with it the decline of the feudal system that had provided Europe's governing structure for centuries.

In the feudal system, the monarch was considered to own all of the land; this he parceled out to the government of his various lords. He often handed out land, based on oaths of loyalty, to those knights and lords who had earned his favor—called vassals. These lords then gave the land to smaller, less powerful lords, also in exchange for oaths of loyalty. Each lord owed support and services to the one over him, creating a pyramid of power with the king at the top; no lord had the power to command the vassal of his vassal. The landholders paid taxes as needed to their overlords, but more importantly they provided troops to support the overlord during times of war.

While kings and lords parceled out the land, many of the people who lived on the lands so parceled were regarded as part of the property. Peasant freemen were granted smaller lots, while the serfs—people who were neither officially slaves nor quite free, and who often were slaves in all respects but the name—provided much of the labor in exchange for the lord's protection. Each piece of land—each manor—was a small, self-sufficient community. The political economy of the day was based not on money but on exchanges of services among the layers of the feudal system.

However, in Chaucer's time, Europe was experiencing a change in climate, with longer, colder winters and cooler, wetter summers. In order to adjust to the seasonal changes, farmers needed to begin the long, devastating process of changing their growing strategies. As famine and disease swept through the population, few people were left to work the land. Landlords began to ask for money instead of services as their payment for food, and they began to pay wages for labor. The feudal system began to fall apart.

The common diet in fourteenth-century England consisted mainly of grains, with very few sources of protein. The people ate some poultry, and an occasional egg, but they rarely, if ever, drank milk. Often undernourished, many people suffered from an increased susceptibility to disease. Those who were unable to subsist in the country moved to London, in hope of finding better conditions. Instead, they arrived to a city whose streets became more and more crowded and dirty, creating the ideal living conditions for the rats that bred the Plague.

The Black Death was really two plagues combined: the bubonic plague, which caused high fevers and nasty swellings, and the subsequent pneumonic plague, which settled in the lungs and almost always brought death. The very young and the very old were among the most susceptible, and these two groups suffered the heaviest casualties. After the first wave of the Black Death hit Europe, an estimated 25 million people were dead—between one third and one fourth of the total population. Due to the overcrowded living conditions, the Plague hit London harder than it did the surrounding countryside—but even so, a thousand English villages disappeared during the Plague's fifty-year ebb and flow. Many historians consider the Black Death the greatest single disaster in European history. It marked the end of the Middle Ages, and it changed the shape of the world forever. The medieval political system of knights and lords and fiefdoms simply could not hold up under the strain of famine and disease on such a scale.

Still, because healthy adults enjoyed a greater immunity to the pestilence, business tended to continue as usual. Schools closed down, but mercantile, legal, and ecclesiastical affairs often went on undisturbed. But the overwhelming presence of death and disease means that Chaucer would have grown up in a world of uncertainty—and therefore of superstition and fear. Torture and execution were common occurrences at the time; the found-guilty were hanged, beheaded, drawn and quartered, burned at the stake, or even blinded, all in public. Corpses were generally left in public squares to serve as examples.

Domestic life was only slightly more genteel. The Byzantine fork was gaining acceptance at a snail's pace among the wealthy in Italy—and the fork was ridiculed when it made its first appearance in England in the early seventeenth century. Spoons of brass and pewter were just on the brink of ubiquity; unlike the knives that always had been in general use as dining utensils, it was usually a host's duty to provide the more common spoons of wood or horn. The wealthy alone, like Chaucer's family, had windows of glass, while the poorer people had only parchment-covered apertures or wooden shutters. Even in the homes of the most affluent, the only places to sit down were benches or cushioned trunks. Lacking insulation, the walls of even the most luxurious houses were cold and damp, and the floors were strewn with straw or reeds to soak up the refuse of various kinds.

The notion of privacy did not have much of a presence. The poor often lived in one room with their livestock. And while the wealthy families had large houses with many rooms, most members spent their time together in the central great hall and then slept several to a bed.

Outside the houses, the streets were narrow, dark, and full of crime. Many people firmly believed that ghosts and demons walked the dark alleys, and few went out at night if it could be avoided. Since candles were expensive, it was customary to go to bed at dusk and rise at the break of dawn. The life expectancy for children was short, and they were affected largely according to their worth as workers. The Church maintained that children were inherently wicked and that it was often necessary to beat the Devil out of them. Priests proclaimed that to "spare the rod" was to "spoil the child."

Without a doubt, stories were the primary means of entertainment for all classes, people often spent what leisure time they had retelling tales. From the country, particularly the North, came stories of the supernatural; miracles were common in the general belief system and even an integral part of the cult of monarchy. Consecrated items were believed to possess properties that were magical or miraculous, depending on the source; it is known that some crumbled the Host over their gardens to kill caterpillars and that others used holy water as a love potion, to kill grasshoppers, or to drive away ghosts.

The Church would have played a large role in Chaucer's childhood. He probably was schooled in the church's vestry, where he would have learned manners, prayers, hymns, and to read and write in Latin. The last of these would have required the help of a hornbook, a piece of parchment covered by a transparent slice of horn. On the parchment was written the alphabet, the Lord's Prayer (in Latin), and some other items of use to the beginning learner. The student was taught all his lessons in French, a language that had been *de rigeur* throughout England since the Norman Conquest in the eleventh century, and that nearly all members of the emerging middle class knew how to speak. After the basic skills of reading and writing would have come the Psalter, where the student learned more complicated Latin.

When the first wave of the plague was over, the Chaucers moved back to London. There Geoffrey began to study at a cathedral school, where he would have had access to a collection of the Latin classics and studied grammar, logic, and rhetoric. Grammar classes taught the parts of speech in Latin, and focused on translation of Latin works into English; also of importance was exegesis—the search for symbolic meaning, particularly Biblical meaning, in literature.

Chaucer's studies in logic would have taught him to analyze argumentation. As a part of these studies, he would have encountered the writings of Aristotle, Boethius, and Macrobius—including works on astrology and alchemy, both common subjects at the time. Chaucer's education would also have extended to arithmetic, physics, and harmony and musical relationships, a subject that included everything from the notes on the scale to the correspondence of the angels and the planets.

The third area of study to which Chaucer would likely have been exposed during his ecclesiastical schooling, rhetoric, was also called "eloquence." It concerned making arguments in prose or poetry that would not only persuade the reader but entertain him as well. The student studied rhyme and other elements of verse; these were considered to have a mystical relationship to each other that went far beyond technique.

To the people of the time, all things in the world were connected to all other things through inscrutable but divine relationships, or correspondences. Everything—from the position of the planets to the shape of a plant—had a significance below the surface that was both spiritual and practical. Chaucer's work reflects a considerable, even burning, curiosity about these relationships and meanings.

The Countess and the King: Chaucer as Page and Prisoner of War

In April of 1357, when he was 14, Chaucer received clothing—a short jacket, a pair of red and black hose, and a pair of shoes—from Elizabeth de Burgh, hereditary Countess of Ulster and wife of Edward III's son Lionel of Antwerp. The Countess, in whose household Chaucer was serving as a page, sent him another set of clothes a few months later and then, at Christmas, money for "necessities".

Chaucer's middle-class blood precluded his rising beyond a certain rank, so he was an assistant or companion to Lionel of Antwerp, later Duke of Clarence, who was only five or so years older than was Chaucer himself. This position afforded Chaucer the opportunity to listen in the evenings as the courtiers entertained the household with music, poetry, wit, and conversation. He even made attempts at musical composition. As a member of Elizabeth's household, he would have been expected to continue his studies, especially in the arts and in French and Latin literature, in the belief that learning of this sort would make a more *refined* servant and thus a more *useful* one. He worked as a scrivener, writing the Countess's correspondence and recording other facts and statistics as necessary.

Chaucer's position with the Countess also would have exposed him to spectacle. In this period, lavish celebrations took place on holy days, including feasting and entertainments. Guests arrived at the castle days before the event and stayed for weeks on end. Celebrations, spanning several days to a week, would include dazzling decorations, costumes, and skilled performances by acrobats and magicians. The men would hunt the meat for the feast, and the tables would be heavy with food, sometimes displayed to look like a miniature landscape, with forests, bridges, and castles with tiny horsemen. Before the feast began, the miniature castles would be burned for the amusement of the guests.

The connections Chaucer gained among the nobility while working for and living with the Countess would help him to gain prestige and influence later in life. The most important of these is undoubtedly John of Gaunt (1340–1399), the fourth son of Edward III and Queen Philippa, and the most powerful lord of his day. Gaunt held the title of Earl of Richmond from birth and many other titles through marriage, including Duke of Lancaster from his first wife and King of Castile and Leon from his second. Gaunt and Chaucer seem to have grown close quickly, and by all evidence they remained close throughout their lives.

Geoffrey also met the King. Modern historians do not think much of Edward III, but Chaucer and his fellow citizens revered him. Edward believed war to be the answer to England's problems, and the English trusted that he was right. Under Edward's leadership, England's army, led by his knights, became known for its might. Though disease and disappointing harvest had struck England, the land's citizens could still pride themselves on military power.

In 1359, still in his adolescence, Chaucer went to war. King Edward had always claimed that he should have inherited the crown of France from his mother, Queen Isabella, the daughter of a French king; and now Edward decided it was time to set things right. While he held the French king hostage in London, he began mustering his troops, and in October he sent nearly a 100,000 thousand men across the English Channel—thus, incidentally, beginning the Hundred Years' War. Among this army was Geoffrey Chaucer.

The wing of the army in which Chaucer traveled saw little action. They marched through land that was already burned and lifeless, thanks to earlier English invasions, and the men began to run out of food. While on a foraging mission, Chaucer was captured by the French and held for ransom.

The King himself paid some of the ransom, which totaled some £16, and his son Edward, the Black Prince, put up most of the rest. After his release, Chaucer again served Lionel of Antwerp, by relaying messages across the Channel.

England returned victorious shortly after Christmas, although the army had actually accomplished very little. Treaty negotiations dragged on after the war; eventually Edward agreed to send the French king home for a ransom of £30 million, but England never saw much of the money. Edward, furious, was about to mount another attack on Paris when his army was struck by a violent storm. Lightning and enormous hailstones killed or injured some 1,000 knights and 6,000 horses. To Edward, this was a sign from God; the English renounced all claim to the French throne. Later, too much later, Edward would rethink this position; but the war with France would drag on throughout the rest of his reign.

The lull in the fighting meant Chaucer was free to follow his own interest, and such history as we have finds him among books.

THE HYPOCRISY OF FRIARS AND THE BLISS OF THE MARRIED: CHAUCER'S POETIC ROOTS

Libraries were not the only place where Chaucer could further his literary studies, however. Poetry in his day was far more important than it is today, and poems were meant to be heard rather than read. Poetry readings were a popular form of entertainment that took place anywhere from the royal palace to country inns. These poems were long and full of romance, adventure, and philosophy.

The next six years were Chaucer's poetic apprenticeship. He spent much of his time listening to poetry read in the royal courts and noble manors, studying not only the structure of the poems themselves but also the way that their authors presented the words to their audiences, the rise and fall of voices, the gestures and inflections.

In the Middle Ages, the first step in a poet's career was to translate and imitate the great poems of earlier centuries, especially the Greek and Roman works of Antiquity. Chaucer began by translating the enormously influential French *Le Roman de la rose* (*The Romance of the*

Rose). He learned much from his work on this translation—allegorical technique, organization of a lengthy and complex work, creating a sense of reality through detail. Most of all, he found his own voice—a unique way of expressing himself with words. By the end of this six-year period, the death of Blanche of Lancaster, John of Gaunt's first wife, inspired Chaucer to produce the protracted elegy *The Book of the Duchess*—a poem still considered a masterpiece.

But during this period Chaucer was not only studying and writing poetry, he was also studying law; a record still exists that refers to Chaucer as a law student. We can infer from the same record that Chaucer was no serious, mild-tempered academic: he was fined two shillings for getting in a fight with a friar. In general, friars of the fourteenth century were not always friends to the people; although these "men of God" made oaths of poverty, they often accumulated wealth from the gifts they received through courting royalty.

Originally, the friars were meant to be homeless, itinerant clergymen who assisted the masses as necessary. They were meant to live so completely on the generosity of others that they were forbidden to touch money. By the fourteenth century, however, many had become corrupt, circumnavigating the rules about money by wearing gloves or having their servants handle the money. Some of them had been gifted scholars, of course, but by Chaucer's day most were poorly educated, and in general the reputation of the friar was at a point among its lowest. In *The Canterbury Tales*, Chaucer would describe a friar as corrupt and hypocritical; we can only assume that the friar involved in Chaucer's "incident" was an early model.

In the Middle Ages, university students were often involved in fights; Oxford was famous for its student riots. The most famous of these, called the Great Slaughter, occurred in 1355, when some students expressed their dislike for a certain tavern keeper's wine. The tavern keeper snapped back at them, and the students threw a wine pot at his head. Soon, the church and university bells were ringing, calling both the villagers and the students to take up their weapons. The brawl lasted two days, and 65 students were killed.

In act, brawls were a common part of life in the fourteenth century. The dagger was a part of the everyday attire of all boys over age 14, and street fights were common, and not always unwelcome, diversions. In fact, it was not unusual for bystanders to watch a street brawl from windows above, or even to shoot an arrow into the fray. Chaucer himself was not a habitual brawler; he had a reputation for being gentle and calm.

Because of his small crime, however, we have a historical record that Chaucer was a law student at this time. Law courses at the time were thorough and intensive, but they were quite a bit different than those offered by today's law schools. John Fortescue, a man who also studied law in the fourteenth century, described his course of study, so we have a record of what Chaucer's studies were *probably* like. They included not only legal studies but also history and even music and dancing. These were meant to give the scholar—the *male* scholar, as women were excluded—the skills he would need to move freely among the nobility and royalty.

The full course of legal studies took at least 16 years, but Chaucer never completed all of them. He was more interested in using his learning to further his poetry. He applied his studies to the law, his attention to poetry performances, and his reading in classical literature all to his own poetic work. By the time he wrote his first original work, the *Book of the Duchess*, he knew how to weave together allusion, metaphor, and symbolism. This was an elegy for a beautiful woman, but in a larger sense its subject was life itself.

People in the Middle Ages believed, generally speaking, that poetry should deal primarily with human nature and its meaning; the poet's function was to explain humanity's place in the universe. A cornerstone of medieval philosophy's endeavor to understand the world was analogy: if the philosopher could study deeply enough how gold related to lead, then he would also understand how a king was related to his subjects—and from there he might attain the real goal, an understanding of the relationship between God and the created world. A second cornerstone was physical structure: if a drop of water was round, and a planet was round, and the Moon was round, then the universe must also be round—and perhaps all of reality had some essential roundness. Little if any distinction was made between physical reality and emotional/spiritual reality; love was an explanation for the world's functioning, as important and practical as any of Newton's laws are to modern physics. Love, in its larger sense of attraction, caused numerous phenomena: the drawing together of odd and even numbers, the crashing of the waves against the shore, the flying of sparks toward the sky, and the yearning of Man for God. Metaphor was no mere poetic device; it was the paradigm.

A theme of intellectual life in the Middle Ages was interconnectedness—what the modern academic is only beginning to call interdisciplinary study—but informed by the greater strength of religious unity. Chaucer, as an ambitious and dedicated poet, would have studied widely and variously: geometry, astrology, numerology, alchemy, music, mathematics. Echoes of all of these appear in his poetry.

We do have some few facts concerning Chaucer's family life in this period. In 1366, when Chaucer was about 23 years old, his father died. His mother immediately remarried a man who also had amassed wealth in the wine business. In the same year, Chaucer too was married. His bride, Philippa Roet, was noble-born, one of the Queen's maidens. Her social position was considerably above Chaucer's, a circumstance that leads some scholars to see in the match the hand of John of Gaunt.

John of Gaunt continued to be a loyal friend to Chaucer. He helped to advance his friend's career in the King's service, and he ensured Chaucer's financial security. Years later, Gaunt would marry his long-time love interest, Katherine Swynford, the widowed sister of Chaucer's wife, and the two men were related officially. Although they were in some ways very different—one a prince and one a talented commoner—the two friends shared intellectual interests and a strong sense of justice. Their lives seem always to have been closely interwoven.

Most historians do not doubt the friendship between Chaucer and John of Gaunt, but many have questioned whether the relationship between Geoffrey and Philippa was as happy. They were frequently apart from each other when Geoffrey was traveling for business reasons, and at one point they maintained separate households. This was a fairly common practice for wealthy people in the Middle Ages, however, and Geoffrey was a busy man who could not help being away from home often on the King's business.

The majority of Chaucer scholars find evidence in Chaucer's work of his own happy marriage. In his poem *The House of Fame*, Chaucer gently mocks the *Divina Commedia*, Dante's tale of elevation to Heaven through an exalted spiritual love for his Beatrice; in fact, Dante saw Beatrice only once or twice. The love in the *Commedia* is constructed not through everyday experience, then, but rather through idealization, through *representation*. Chaucer's work, on the contrary, suggests that the ordinary, commonplace love of a husband for a wife may save the soul at least as well as Dante's ethereal love for Beatrice. In *The Book of the Duchess*, Chaucer suggests that a woman's love brings salvation, and his poetry frequently compares the happiness of marriage to the happiness of Heaven. He often compares marital love to God's love for humanity. It is from these representations of love that scholars derive their belief that Chaucer's marriage was a happy one; but in any case he and Philippa had three children together (Elizabeth, Thomas, and Lewis).

While Chaucer's home life may have been stable and contented, though, the world around him was full of upheaval and strife. England was still at war, against both France and the Black Death.

DARK DAYS FOR ENGLAND

When John of Gaunt led troops against France, Chaucer rode with him, leaving his wife to attend to John's mother, the Queen.

In England, abnormally heavy rains brought floods and disease. The royal court tried to seal itself off from the rest of London, but they could not escape; the Queen herself became ill. Chaucer's wife stood by and watched while the royal physicians bled the Queen, hoping to drain the poison from her. Perhaps owing to their efforts, the Queen died in short order. When John of Gaunt heard that his mother had died, he was plunged into grief, but still he had to attend to the war against France. He returned to England for his mother's funeral, and then, once again accompanied by Chaucer, he led another military expedition across the Channel. Gaunt's wife, Blanche, traveled with him; part of Chaucer's job was to entertain her with poetry and conversation.

The Duchess and her ladies were settled in a castle in the countryside, where they hoped they would be secure from the Black Death, which was spreading through France's cities as well as England's. The Plague did strike the castle, though, and Blanche was not spared. The Black Prince, John of Gaunt's older brother and the heir to the throne, also was wasting away from illness. He would soon die, too. Chaucer's *Book of the Duchess* may have been an attempt at consolation—certainly, at consolation for the loss of Blanche—but nevertheless John's campaign against France faltered.

In 1366, England stepped in to circumvent a storm that was brewing in Spain. That country's ruler, Pedro I ("the Cruel"), had committed various atrocities, including some against a French princess, and France had launched an attack and gained the Spanish throne. Pedro sought England's aid. Regardless of its opinion of Pedro's actions,

England certainly did not want France to take all of Spain—so Edward, the Black Prince, took to Spain an army and a group of diplomats, including Chaucer. The expedition succeeded in restoring Pedro I to his throne and then returned to France; Pedro recommenced the acts on which his reputation had been founded.

In 1372, John of Gaunt made a political marriage with Constance, a daughter of this same Pedro. Thus Gaunt became the legal king of Leon and Castile, even though he had fallen in love with the sister of Chaucer's wife—Katherine Swynford—whom he kept as a mistress and by whom he had several children. Another quarter-century would pass before Constance's death would enable John of Gaunt to become Chaucer's brother in a legally sanctioned way.

The royal affairs at home in England were similarly complicated. Now that the Queen had died, King Edward also took a mistress, Alice Perrers. Like Katherine Swynford, Alice was a commoner, no fitting candidate for the throne, but her influence over the King became so great as to make her the *de facto* monarch of England.

Chaucer and Alice were good friends. They came from similar backgrounds, and they had probably served together for years in the royal court. Alice had been one of the Queen's ladies, her favorite and best loved, in fact. The Queen requested in her will, ironically or sincerely, that the King take care of "our beloved damsel Alicia."

Alice may have been an ambitious and powerful woman, but she also seems to have truly loved the king, at least in the beginning. John of Gaunt and Chaucer apparently thought well of her, for the most part. She was a good friend to Chaucer, and his success was partly due to her support.

During Alice's time of power, Chaucer also grew in influence and prestige. It was during this time that he made his first trip to Italy, and he was rewarded for all his efforts for the crown with a house and more opportunities to advance himself. Given Alice's influence over the king, if she had not liked him, Chaucer would not have been able to experience such success. Alice was an intelligent and humorous woman who no doubt enjoyed Chaucer's quick intellect. The feeling was probably mutual.

Chaucer could not approve of all that Alice did, however. As Edward III grew older and began to lose his faculties, Alice began to take advantage of him, siphoning money from the royal accounts and taking for herself all of the dead queen's jewels. The King was so oblivious to her schemes that he held a huge seven-day celebration in her honor, calling her "the Lady of the Sun." Such an enormous event was obviously expensive, and it came at a time when England's financial situation was desperate. Londoners were tired and angry, sick of the endless taxes they paid to support the royal household. In the "Good Parliament" of 1376, Alice was stripped of all her honors and removed from Edward's court.

Both Chaucer and John of Gaunt were furious. They may not have approved of all of Alice's plots, but they also believed firmly in the King's "ancient right." They did not think that any parliament had the right to meddle in a king's personal business, and they feared that if Parliament were allowed such power it would bring an end to the strength of England's centralized government. Alice's actions had made her symbolically vulnerable to Parliament's own ends, though, and Gaunt and Chaucer could do little to protect her.

Chaucer did what he could for her with his poetry. Alice served as the inspiration for his Wife of Bath, Dame Alice, in *The Canterbury Tales.* Like Alice Perrers, the Wife of Bath is described as intelligent, shameless, greedy, funny, and ambitious. She claims that women should have a voice in their own affairs; through and across her flaws, she is strong and charismatic. Whether Chaucer intended the Wife of Bath to be a private joke between him and his audience is uncertain, but his portrayal of Alice *was* humorous and sympathetic, and it may well have helped her to win some leniency.

In any event, the sympathetic portrayal of Alice Perrers—if this is what it is—seems to have had no ill effect on Chaucer's own career, which continued to flourish. He had chosen his friends wisely, and he seems to have been careful to avoid trouble.

CHAUCER'S FAVOR WITH THE KING; CHAUCER'S POLITICS

Soon after Chaucer's return from the diplomatic voyage to Italy in 1374, he was granted a free lifetime lease to a house that was near his new job as Controller of the Customs. This job meant that he kept the records for the port of London, a prestigious and lucrative responsibility. The same year, John of Gaunt awarded to him a pension of £10 per annum. On Saint George's Day, Chaucer was given the reward of a pitcher of wine daily for life.

Saint George's Day was a religious celebration, but it was also the special day of the knights' Order of the Garter. The Garter knights were wealthy men, and their celebration would have been sumptuous, with everyone, including Geoffrey Chaucer, dressed in all their jewels and furs. Chaucer was by this time considered to be a sort of government ornament; his talent and intellect proved the royal court's worth, and his performance of a new poem at the Saint George's Day festivities would have held a central place in the celebration. If he did write a poem in honor of this day, it has not survived, but historians assume that he received the pitcher of wine for life as a reward for his skill in presenting this lost poem. A few years later, he converted this honorary gift to cash, adding to his already comfortable wealth.

Chaucer's life was certainly a comfortable one, but his job as Controller of the Customs was not merely honorary; he truly had to work hard, and his work was of utmost importance to the government's finances. Customs collection was the crown's main source of revenue, but many of the collectors in London were known to be both powerful and crooked. Surrounded by this sort of dishonesty, Chaucer would have been in an awkward position. He would also have faced great temptation to engage in his own surreptitions. Whether he did so is unknown.

Chaucer was a survivor. He had seen some of his friends and fellow poets speak out against government corruption, and he knew how little their efforts had accomplished. In fact, some of them had been hanged for their efforts. Chaucer's seems to have waited for events to run their course.

His job may have had certain tensions, but his new house was truly a mansion. His grant for the house gave him "the whole dwelling house above Aldgate Gate, with the chambers thereon built and a certain cellar beneath the said gate, on the eastern side thereof, together with all its appurtenances, for the lifetime of said Geoffrey." The house had once been used as a prison, but in the same grant officials promised that they would no longer house prisoners there. The house was splendidly furnished, and John of Gaunt helped to make it even more luxurious by giving expensive cups to Philippa Chaucer as New Year's gifts in 1380, 1381, and 1382. She must have been able to entertain in style, thanks to the Duke's generosity. Chaucer also kept his personal library in the house—60 books in all, an enormous collection for the time.

By this point, Chaucer was firmly established as a loyal and valuable servant of the government. He had a dual role at court: first as a poet and second as a government employee. As a sign of the royal esteem, Chaucer was frequently sent abroad on the king's business during the next few years. Someone else served in his place as Controller while he was gone. Most of his missions involved peace treaties and marriage agreements.

Edward had finally realized the importance of bringing an end to the long war with France. His own health was slipping, and as the feudal system fell apart in England, the peasants began to complain about the endless fighting. Riots among the common people were becoming more and more frequent, and meanwhile the King was more dependent on the commoners for his funds. Just as Parliament had stepped in to put an end to Alice Perrer's costly schemes, now Parliament tried to control the King's expenses. Chaucer was outraged, and he expressed his feelings in his poetry. But he also understood that the King needed to bring an end to the same war that Chaucer had once supported.

To achieve peace with France, Chaucer was sent on a delicate diplomatic mission: the arrangement of a marriage between Edward's grandson Richard and the daughter of the King of France. Chaucer was tactful and skilled in persuasion, but the marriage commission ultimately failed: in the final stages of negotiation, the young princess died. Chaucer and the other diplomats with him tried to work out a substitute agreement with the French king's second daughter, but the French suddenly withdrew from the discussion. They were no longer interested in pursuing the alliance.

Almost immediately, Chaucer was sent on another marriage mission; this time he was ordered to arrange a marriage for Prince Richard with the daughter of the duke of Milan. The idea now was to gain an alliance with this Italian state, to increase England's strength against France. However, again the mission proved unsuccessful, and Chaucer made the long trip back home to England. He must have been relieved to get back to his library and his poetry.

As busy as he was with his job and his royal missions, Chaucer was continuing to read and write throughout this period of his life, although historians are not certain exactly which poems he wrote when. He probably, however, wrote *The Parliament of Fowls* sometime during these years.

Parliament expresses Chaucer's disapproval of the House of Commons. Although today we may not be able to understand his point of view, Chaucer was a political conservative, resistant to change. He did not want to see the king's authority diminished; Chaucer's close friendship with John of Gaunt, a king's son, may have had something to do with his loyalty. In any event, *The Parliament of Fowls* is a satire that pokes fun at the parliamentary procedure exercised by the House of Commons.

During these years, Chaucer wrote "The Monk's Tale," which would eventually become a part of *The Canterbury Tales*. Like *Parliament*, "The Monk's Tale" expresses Chaucer's scorn for disrespectful and unruly commoners.

Both "The Monk's Tale" and *Parliament of Fowls* also demonstrate the influence of Italian poetry on Chaucer's work. His visits to Italy had shown him a new way of handling the old classic stories; instead of using the various characters simply as symbols to express some universal moral, the Italian authors were writing histories of men's lives, histories that focused as much on the various individuals' qualities and unique accomplishments as on the "moral of the story." Chaucer was obviously fascinated and delighted by the individual quirks and deeds of his characters, and he applied this fascination and delight to his poetry. His readers must have been startled and intrigued by the way he brought a gossipy, contemporary feel to the old classic stories. Although "The Monk's Tale" is considered to be one of Chaucer's less successful poems, in it, as in all his writing, Chaucer demonstrates his understanding of what real people might actually say and feel.

All of Chaucer's work, at whatever point in his life, has a common characteristic: a tension between opposite perspectives on life. On the one hand, Chaucer saw life from a Christian philosophical point of view. On the other hand, he always felt sympathy with—even delight in—the sins and foibles of ordinary people. Throughout his life, he was never able to unify these two points of view in his poetry, but many literary critics feel that is part of Chaucer's charm. Perhaps he could not reconcile these two perspectives in his poetry because he could not completely reconcile them in his own life.

However, throughout his life he firmly supported an absolute and unchallenged royalty. Dante put it this way: "The one will that resolves the many." In Chaucer's mind, and in the minds of others like him in the fourteenth century, a monarch's function was to provide the country with this "one will." Instead, as the common people grew in power, Chaucer saw a growing "manyness" replacing the royal "oneness." He seems not to have recognized that his own work, which expresses an obvious affection and respect for common people, reflected this new way of thinking.

Turmoil in England: John Wyclif and the Church; John Ball and the Peasants' Revolt

While Chaucer was away on yet another diplomatic mission, the whole shape of England's government suddenly changed. On June 21, 1377, Edward III died at Sheen Palace in Surrey. On July 16, his young grandson Richard—the son of Edward, the Black Prince, who had died in 1376—was crowned King of England, as his grandfather had been, at Westminster Abbey.

Richard was only 10 years old, but his coronation filled England with a new hope. All of England's terrible problems would be over now, people believed, and to express their conviction that all would be well, they threw the young king a coronation party like none other. A monk of Evesham who kept a chronicle of the event recorded that the coronation was "celebrated with great ceremony of a sort never seen anywhere before, in the presence of archbishops, bishops, other prelates of the Church, and all the magnates of his realm."

Edward's long and expensive wars had nearly destroyed England, and under his rule England had become a place of rebellion and suspicion. John of Gaunt, the new king's uncle, hoped to use Richard to unite the kingdom and put an end to the commoners' growing influence. Gaunt also wanted to curtail the vast and often corrupt power of the Church, which also posed a threat to the centralization of power; so he supported the religious reformer John Wyclif. Today, Wyclif is remembered for being the first to translate the Bible into English, the vernacular of his day, which had begun to replace French in legal proceedings in 1362. This first translation owes its existence to Wyclif's proto-Protestant conviction that ordinary people should be able to read the Bible for themselves and should not have to depend on the interpretation of the Church.

Wyclif believed strongly that the Pope and the Church should have less power. He saw faith as deeply personal and based solely on individual interpretation of Scripture. John of Gaunt had a deep respect for this bespectacled, soft-spoken scholar, a respect that transcended Wyclif's usefulness in Gaunt's own plans. But Wyclif *was* useful to

Gaunt, because Wyclif preached openly against ecclesiastical control of secular government.

The English bishops were infuriated by Wyclif's sermons, and they began to mount an attack against him. Wyclif did not believe in some basic Church tenets—he did not, for example, believe in transubstantiation, i.e. that during the rite of Communion the bread and wine became the actual body and blood of Christ, as the Church taught—and the bishops thought they would be able to convict Wyclif of heresy.

John of Gaunt had openly supported and encouraged Wyclif, so when Wyclif was brought to trial Gaunt knew that he too was partially responsible for Wyclif's predicament. Gaunt traveled through London raising support for Wyclif, and then he broke into the trial with the support of a troop of armed men. He had no official authority to interrupt the proceedings, but through his intervention Wyclif was saved from burning at the stake.

Traveling in continental Europe, Chaucer heard the rumors about his friend. Chaucer too sympathized with Wyclif's position, and Chaucer secretly applauded John of Gaunt's actions. Both Chaucer and Gaunt wanted to rebuild the feudal system, which was based on a specific idea of courtesy—that government should be held together by a chain of esteem and dependence that began with the monarch and extended to the lowest serf. Chaucer would elaborate on this belief a few years later in *The Legend of Good Women.* Chaucer and Gaunt seem both to have believed truly that as moral men they needed a king who would rule the nation with a total unifying power.

Gaunt and Chaucer had great hopes that young Richard would be able to accomplish their goal of bringing the throne back to power, but he was only a child, crowned at ten years of age, too young to understand the kingdom's deep-seated problems. He had no strength of his own; he had to depend on his counselors and advisers.

Meanwhile, diplomacy, presumably including Chaucer's own constant missions, was unsuccessful. The war with France continued, and England's situation became even more desperate. The monk of Evesham, who had kept a chronicle of Richard's coronation, wrote these words in the first year of Richard's rule:

> In this year there was a complete collapse of peace nego-
> tiations ... the French landed on the Isle of Wight.... [W]hen

they had looted and set fire to several places, they took a thousand marks as ransom for the island. Then they returned to the sea and sailed along the English coastline continuously until Michaelmas. They burnt many places and killed, especially in the southeastern areas, all the people they could find. As they met with little resistance they carried off animals and other goods as well as several prisoners. It is believed that at this time more evils were perpetrated than had been caused by enemy attacks on England during the previous forty years.

Chaucer's writings never comment directly on this time of fear. His *Canterbury Tales*, however, may reflect his feelings about the atmosphere of distrust and division that existed in England during these years.

Not only did England have to continue to fight against a foreign enemy, but now it had to fight a growing rebellion at home as well. A new idea—really, an old idea that had been forgotten—was gaining enthusiasts in the lower classes: that all men had rights. The peasants were becoming angrier each year about the heavy taxes that kept them poor; the serfs who were still tied to the land wanted wages for their work; and the common people blamed the government for all the kingdom's many recent disasters. All saw in Gaunt a symbol of their problems.

A priest named John Ball began to incite revolt among the peasants. Meetings were held across England, secret messages were passed back and forth, and inflammatory sermons were preached. Ball—"the mad priest of Kent"—did everything he could to fan the sparks of peasant rebellion into flame. His goal was to murder the royal ministers, especially John of Gaunt, and then parcel the land among the poor.

In the spring of 1381, Ball succeeded. His accusations of corruption among the King's ministers caused the masses to attack all officials they could find, and many royal ministers were beheaded in the tumult. Chaucer either was not present for these events or escaped unharmed. John of Gaunt too survived, although the rebels destroyed his house. The commoners hated him; they saw him as indifferent to their grievances. In fact, though, both he and Chaucer seem to have cared sincerely about the welfare of the poor. The peasants loved King Richard, and the boy king was able to bring the fighting to a close.

Nevertheless, the pall of suspicion remained over England, and the general feeling about government officials was a direct threat to Chaucer and his family, particularly considering his friendship with John of Gaunt. Meanwhile, he was also in financial difficulties: the government was reluctant to pay him for his assignments. But Chaucer was not poor; his income was considerable, and he was paid a sizable stipend for the care of two wealthy, orphaned wards.

In fact, some literary critics have accused Chaucer of being *too* comfortable. They point out that while England was being torn apart Chaucer seems to have watched passively, rather than committing passionately to one side or another. Other critics defend Chaucer, saying that, given his political beliefs, his poetry expresses a surprising sympathy for all the classes. Throughout his poetry, he appeals for justice and reason to prevail on behalf of rich and poor, noble and common, male and female, and he chides the politics of extremists like John Ball. It is rare to see a subject in Chaucer's work taken seriously; rather, the tendency is to satirize viewpoints that differ from his own. Chaucer's reference to the Peasants' Revolt in "The Nun's Priest's Tale" as "terrible yelling of fiends in hell" may seem judgemental, but Chaucer often used exaggeration and irony to explore complex or ambiguous issues. His political thought defies any definition based on a single citation from his work.

But for all Chaucer's reasonable defense of human rights, he hated the technique of the revolt. He believed that no matter how legitimate their objections, people should accept their positions in life and submit to authority. If authority became corrupt—and he knew that it often did—then the people should not attempt to fix it but should wait for it to fix itself. Chaucer seems to have believed firmly that this was God's will for human beings, and no matter how sympathetic he was of the peasants as individuals, he hated the violence they had caused.

Perhaps to escape the threat of this very violence, in 1381 Chaucer sold his family home. He still lived in Aldgate, and he kept his position as Controller, but now someone else held the same post as well, and he was freed from the job's daily responsibilities.

By this time, King Richard was happily married to Anne of Bohemia, and Chaucer no longer needed to run around Europe trying to work out marriage contracts; he could stay at home with Philippa for a few years and concentrate on his poetry and his studies. During these years he translated some older poems into English and worked on *Troilus and Criseyde*, one of his masterpieces. He also wrote *The House of Fame* and *The Legend of Good Women* during this time. He was popular in Richard's court, and Queen Anne especially loved his poetry, finding it sympathetic to women.

As always, Chaucer was wholly loyal to the monarch. Still, some historians wonder whether he is referring to King Richard when in *Troilus and Criseyde* he comments on Troilus's extreme melancholy that eventually becomes rage and revenge. As he grew into a man, King Richard showed the same kind of neurotic depression. He was obsessed with his murdered great-grandfather, Edward II, and he tried to pattern himself after Edward in every possible way.

THE LOSS AND RESTORATION OF ROYAL FAVOR; LIFE IN THE COUNTRY

The young king who had been crowned with such hope was becoming erratic. Aside from his emotional extremes, he was proving to be as extravagant as his grandfather had been. Parliament and his uncles— including John of Gaunt—tried to control his spending, but they had little success. Richard continued to hand out enormous, expensive gifts to everyone he liked, apparently with no understanding of England's financial situation. The kind may call him generous, but his generosity seems to have been shortsighted and selfish.

John of Gaunt was searching desperately for a solution to England's problems. War was the traditional answer when a country was in financial difficulties, since a successful war provided new land and ransom money for the upper classes and spoils to the lower classes. Moreover, it turned people's attention away from domestic problems and encouraged patriotism.

Gaunt knew that to continue his father's war against France was a hopeless cause that would only end in England's quicker ruin, but he decided that battling Portugal stood a greater chance of success. Even better, between September of 1378 and June of 1379 the Church was divided by the Western Schism, as both Robert of Geneva (Clement VII) and Bartolomeo Prignano (Urban VI) claimed with various support the papal throne. Clement enjoyed the backing of all of western Europe, excluding Ireland, England, and the English regions of France, and Urban held most of Germany, Flanders, and all of Italy with the exception of Naples. As Portugal supported Clement, supporters of Urban might easily consider war against Portugal a holy crusade.

In the end, though, Gaunt could not raise support for his plan. Instead, the bishops of England came up with another idea: a "glorious crusade" to Europe to "persuade" people, through military force, to accept Urban as the rightful pope. In reality, this was a fund-raiser. The crusade was financed by Pope Urban's sale of plenary remissions: for a certain sum of money, Urban would forgive the sins of a given soul, living or dead. (Angels from heaven, claimed adherents of this system, would come down to bring souls out of purgatory and carry them into the skies.) Needless to say, the idea was attractive to the guilty conscience, and plenary remissions became a major source of income.

John of Gaunt was indignant, as was John Wyclif. Chaucer saw all too clearly how ridiculous the plan was: Urban was selling something imaginary, or at least something that he had no power to grant, for large sums of very real gold. He listened to the claims of Urban's supporters with a cynical amusement that he expressed in the prologue to *The Canterbury Tales*, describing the "gentle Pardoner of Rouncivale":

> But none was as crafty, from Berwyck to Ware
> Nor was there another such pardoner.
> For in his suit of mail he had a pillowcase
> Which he said was Our Lady's veil;
> He said he a chunk of the sail
> From Saint Peter's boat used for his trade
> Upon the sea, until he went when Jesus Christ bade.
> He had a cross of false gold full of stones,
> And in a glass he had pig bones.
> But with these relics, whenever he found
> A poor person dwelling upon the land,
> He would get himself more money
> Than that poor person could earn in months twenty....

Chaucer's opinion of plenary remissions is clear.

In any case, the "glorious crusade" was no more successful than anything else. England's military and political power was diminished by it rather than increased, and it did nothing to win support for Urban. Its only positive effect was an increase in Urban's own wealth.

In addition, the young King Richard, now of age, was turning out to be beyond John of Gaunt's control. Chaucer and Gaunt supported a strong and rational royal rule, but Richard's belief in his own power as king was extreme and irrational; in Richard's eyes, his strength was divine, dependent on no one, and he could do whatever he wanted. His uncle's attempts to rein him in resulted only in resentment.

In 1384, a friar named John Latimer told Richard that John of Gaunt was plotting Richard's murder. Richard was prepared to have his uncle hanged immediately, but Parliament listened to Gaunt's defense, investigated, uncovered the plot, and killed the friar. Chaucer took part in these events in no known way, but his work's opinion of meddling friars, combined with his long-lived friendship with John of Gaunt, suggests an acute awareness. Gaunt escaped hanging partly because his brother, the Earl of Gloucester, leaped to his defense. After these events, Gaunt decided to leave England; he took an army and went to claim his legal right to the throne of Castile, leaving his brother, Gloucester, to deal with the King.

With Gaunt out of England, Chaucer found himself in an awkward position. Gaunt had always carefully walked the fine line between controlling the King and giving him his loyalty, but the Earl of Gloucester felt no such scruples. He began to take more and more power for himself, a move that Chaucer could not support.

Gloucester knew that Chaucer supported the King, and during the years of Gloucester's control Chaucer clearly fell out of favor. He gave up his house over Aldgate and his position as Controller of the Customs; he also surrendered his pensions.

However, although Gloucester had no love for Chaucer, Richard was still his friend. Some historians have argued that the King granted Chaucer a better job as steward of some of the royal palaces. These historians believe the records indicate that Chaucer also received a small royal manor in the country, where he took up residence with his family. Certain lines in his poetry are said to support these suppositions. In any event, the poetry written during these years *does* indicate that Chaucer was spending time in the country. He describes nature in great detail: he talks of the little daisy that "upriseth early in the morning, and spreads itself before the sun" and of being down on his knees in grass that was embroidered with flowers, breathing in the sweet scents. The opening lines of the General Prologue to *The Canterbury Tales* and the passages on country life in "The Knight's Tale," "The Miller's Tale," and "The Reeve's Tale," all written about this time, suggest the same delight in nature.

During his time living in the country, Chaucer also became familiar with the country folk he portrayed in *The Canterbury Tales*. His words made these individuals live forever in his readers' imaginations. For all his understanding and sympathy, however, Chaucer always refused to be sentimental about even his most noble or humble characters; he brought his sly, sarcastic humor to everything he wrote.

When Chaucer moved to the country, he probably brought his entire family with him, except for his oldest daughter, who had now joined a convent (generously sponsored by John of Gaunt). Geoffrey's son Thomas was now about 12; he may have spent some of his time at school in London. Soon he would be placed in the household of a great lord, probably Gaunt's, to be trained as a squire. Lewis Chaucer, born in 1380 or so, would have been four or five, and Chaucer may have spent time teaching his young son during these more quiet years. We know from Chaucer's remarks in *Astrolabe* that Lewis was a bright boy who was especially quick at mathematics. Chaucer may have written his book *Sphere*, about the Earth itself, for Lewis.

Lewis and sometimes Thomas probably went with their father when he inspected the workmen on the royal estates. He may have taken them out in a boat with him when he checked the royal dikes and bridges. When they grew up, both boys would be royal stewards, so they certainly followed in their father's footsteps. They were both successful men who must have been loved and encouraged as children.

The health of the children's mother may have been one reason Chaucer moved his family to the country. By now Philippa would have been in her mid-40s, an age that was considered old for a woman in the Middle Ages. She had given up her work as a royal lady in waiting, and she no longer collected a salary from the crown, a hint to historians that her health may have been poor. Women's lives were not easy in the fourteenth century—childbearing wore out their bodies, and living constantly inside buildings that were damp and drafty made them inclined to illness. Three years later she died.

In the meantime, Chaucer was writing more than ever before, and his work reached new heights of skill. Somehow he always managed to balance his family and work responsibilities with his dedication to his poetry. In 1385, Chaucer's responsibilities grew even greater when he was made a justice of the peace.

The justices, however, met only four times a year, so Chaucer's duties, though prestigious, were not heavy. At these sessions, Chaucer's responsibilities would have included arresting offenders, examining them under oath, and then drawing up an indictment for the justice who would hear and determine the case. In this role, Chaucer would have had the opportunity to closely observe all sorts of rascals, from thieves to murderers. In his official capacity, he no doubt was partially responsible for the punishment of these people, but in his writing he was always sympathetic to even the worst scoundrels.

The year after he was appointed as justice of the peace, Chaucer served a term in Parliament. To do so, he had to leave the country and return to London. There he once more had to face the Earl of Gloucester.

Parliament was locked in the battle between Gloucester and the king, and Chaucer once again was forced to keep a low profile to avoid calling Gloucester's attention to himself. Many of Chaucer's associates, men who like him had worked for King Richard, were brutally executed, until the street around the executioner's block was actually shoe-deep in blood. Never before in English history had so many noblemen been put to death for such trivial reasons.

Although Chaucer survived this dangerous time, it was not a pleasant one for him. He was harassed in many small ways that must have exasperated and tired him. He was sued over and over for many small debts, and at the same time he had trouble collecting the annuities that were due to him.

The following year, however, Gloucester's triumph was over, at least for the time being. Richard was now 22, old enough to run the kingdom without any help from his uncles. At a meeting of the great council, he announced his intention of doing so. And later in the same year, John of Gaunt returned home to England.

Once Gloucester was no longer in power, all of Chaucer's privileges and annuities were returned to him. He was made chief clerk of the king's works, an enormous job that put him in charge of many royal properties, including Westminster Palace, the Tower of London, and many other castles and manors. Chaucer supervised the building of things as temporary as tournament scaffolds and as permanent as portions of the Tower and Westminster Abbey. He had the opportunity to choose the architects and leave his mark on the English landscape in a real and lasting way. The bookkeeping alone involved with the position was a full-time job, so it was not an easy job, but it was prestigious and rewarding.

In the course of his work, Chaucer traveled a good deal between 1389 and 1391. The English roads of the time were narrow and crooked, often enclosed by walls or thick trees. Villages were far apart, and gangs of highwaymen ruled the empty spaces between. The danger was not academic; on September 3, 1390, highwaymen in Kent accosted Chaucer, then a stout, middle-aged man. They took from him about £20 and fled. Three days later, Chaucer was traveling the road to Westminster; this time the robbers stole £10. Later in the same month, in Surrey, highwaymen *again* robbed Chaucer. The money stolen from him was the King's, and Chaucer was excused from repaying it. The thieves were eventually caught and brought to justice.

In 1391, he was relieved of his responsibilities and given a position that was far less demanding—steward of the royal forest at Petherton. This was likely an accounting job, involving little labor, and Chaucer now had plenty of undisturbed time to write.

His wife was dead now, and his sons were no longer at home—one at school and one in service for John of Gaunt. Chaucer continued his work on *The Canterbury Tales* and did some of his best writing during the first half of the decade. The century was drawing to a close, however, and with it would end Chaucer's life.

UPHEAVAL AT COURT; CHAUCER'S LAST LOSS OF FAVOR

At first, things seemed to be going well for Chaucer's friends. Richard II had become a popular king. Unlike his grandfather, Richard hated war, and for the first time in years England achieved a lasting peace with France. After Queen Anne's death in 1394, Richard cemented the peace with France by marrying Isabella, the daughter of Charles VI of France.

John of Gaunt's Spanish second wife had also died, leaving him free at last to marry (in 1396) the woman he had loved for years, Katherine Swynford, the sister of Chaucer's wife, Philippa. The two already had children together, and the King now declared these legitimate and rewarded Gaunt for his years of loyalty by enlarging his lands.

But as the new century approached, people began to murmur disturbing gossip about the King. When one of his friends died abroad, the King asked that his coffin be brought to him and opened. According to one observer, he gazed "long and earnestly" at the face of the embalmed corpse, and then clutched the dead hands in his. To both friends and enemies, this must have been odd—still, it was only a rumor. Then, however, the King began to talk endlessly, both in private and in public, about his murdered great-grandfather. He had always been obsessed with Edward II, but now he began to speak of the dead king as a martyred saint. He intentionally carried his imitation of his great-grandfather to ever greater extremes, becoming more and more extravagant, just as Edward II had been. Thomas of Woodstock, Earl of Gloucester, began to talk again of regaining his power.

Now another ugly rumor crept around the court, and this one certainly reached the King's ears: according to the gossip, Gloucester was plotting Richard's assassination. The King retaliated immediately. He invited Gloucester and two of his supporters—Richard Fitzalan, Earl of Arundel, and Thomas de Beauchamp, Earl of Warwick—to one of his extravagant banquets. Citing illness, Gloucester did not attend; Arundel simply stayed home. Warwick, then an old man, accepted the invitation. The two men dined together, and then the King sent Warwick to the Tower. Next on the list were Arundel and Gloucester.

In the end, Arundel was tried for treason and beheaded. Gloucester never had a chance to stand trial. A member of the royalist party, fearing that Richard and Gaunt would never allow their own uncle and brother to be convicted, murdered Gloucester in the Tower; Gloucester was convicted of treason posthumously. When old Warwick was eventually brought in to stand trial, he wailed and whined, according to the chronicler Adam of Usk, "like a wretched old woman." Because he made a full confession of his part in the plot against the King, Richard did not execute him. Instead, he banished Warwick for life to the Isle of Man.

Over the next few months, the King banished his less important enemies, too, and redistributed their land among his supporters. He did all this carefully, strictly observing English law, and for a time he succeeded in regaining his power.

But in time his emotional problems again weakened his rule. According to the chronicler Walsingam, the King now was afraid to go to bed for fear of Arundel's ghost. His actions seemed paranoiac, but after all he had good reason to suspect those around him, as his own uncle had plotted his death. He began to watch his courtiers "like an eagle." Adam of Usk writes that on feast days the King would sit on his throne from dinnertime to Vespers, not speaking to anyone, simply staring from face to face. If someone happened to meet his eyes, that person was required to immediately genuflect, as though in the presence of some holy relic. The King had always believed himself holy, God's direct representative, but now his self-importance grew. At the same time, he began to depend more and more on psychics and soothsayers, who promised him that he would one day be the greatest prince in the world. Chaucer, with his sensible and ironic good humor, must have felt out of place in the royal court during these strange, tense days.

England might have put up with Richard's peculiarities if he had not also become even more extravagant with the court's money. His popularity plunged, and his fear and paranoia increased. For all Chaucer's misgivings, however, he continued to support the king, and late in the century, Richard called him out of retirement to go through England to muster up royal support. Richard himself began to travel as well, accompanied by his army. He took to terrorizing and torturing his enemies to prove his strength, but in the end, his actions only brought about his downfall. England began to hate him.

In 1399, Richard lost his lifetime protector and supporter, and Chaucer lost his oldest friend. John of Gaunt died, leaving his enormous land and wealth to his son, Henry of Bolingbroke.

Henry was no friend of Richard's, and he had been banished along with the king's other enemies. Now, however, he returned to England, accompanied by an invasion force. As he headed toward his father's ancestral castle, huge numbers of common people joined his troops.

They captured Richard and brought him to London. There, Henry was greeted with cheers, while people hooted at Richard as he was carried to the Tower. Gaunt's son Henry became the new king of England. Soon after this, Richard was murdered.

Chaucer's writing of this period is full of protestations that he is no longer able to write as he used to because of his advanced age; his writing *does* change at the time, and he becomes less prolific. Parodying more serious writing, he mocks his loftier sentiments in even the most high-minded stories of *The Canterbury Tales*.

Now that Henry IV was in power, Chaucer for the first time was no longer a king's favorite. Perhaps honoring his father's long friendship with Chaucer, the new king did not retaliate against Chaucer for his support of Richard; but he was never quite as generous with him as former kings had been. Chaucer even had to resort on occasion to writing amusing pleas for the King's generosity. These begging poems were his last works.

Chaucer moved now into a smaller house next to Westminster Abbey. He is said to have become deeply religious in his last year or so, and the story goes that he repented of all that he had written. Many modern historians, however, wonder if this total repentance was not thrust upon Chaucer by the clergy of the day. They point to the fact that throughout his life Chaucer wrote of his confidence in a loving deity. Why, they wonder, would Chaucer have felt such terror as he approached his death that he would have recanted the work that had brought pleasure to so wide an audience?

The exact circumstances of Chaucer's death are unknown; all that is certain is that he died on October 25, 1400. Historians have noted that the Plague struck again in 1400, so perhaps this time, older and less resistant to illness, Chaucer contracted the fatal disease. He was buried in Westminster Abbey, near his house, a place normally reserved for the burial of royalty.

"The Father of English Poetry"

All that we know about Chaucer's life is drawn from the many times his name appears in the business records of his day—and from his own writing. In effect we have a skeleton of his life that historians have fleshed out with clues from Chaucer's work. Scholars do not all agree on the interpretation of the bare facts; for instance, a few historians point out that John of Gaunt and Chaucer may not have been good friends at all. Their names are often linked in the records of the day, John of Gaunt is recorded as giving Chaucer many gifts, and Chaucer often referred to Gaunt as "our beloved" in his writing. But we do not *know* how the two men felt about each other. We can only guess.

His most famous work continues to be the *Canterbury Tales*, a long work he began about 1387 and continued to write for the rest of his life. He originally intended to have 30 pilgrims tell four tales each, two while traveling to Canterbury and two while traveling from Canterbury. However, he had finished only 23 pilgrims' stories before his death.

The *Canterbury Tales* quickly spread throughout England in the early fifteenth century. Scholars feel the stories reached their instant and continued success because of their accurate and often vivid portrayal of human nature. No other English poet was as revered by the people of the day.

When Chaucer wrote his poetry, he "published" it by reading it out loud to gatherings of people at the royal court and for celebrations. No doubt people had their favorites, works that they asked him to read over and over, but they also pressed him for new works. Any time Chaucer was invited to a party, he composed a few lines in honor of the occasion, and for big events he wrote more lengthy works.

Nearly 100 years after Chaucer's death, however, his works were printed for the first time. The first printer of his works, Caxton, described Chaucer as "the worshipful father and first founder and embellisher of ornate eloquence in our English."

Chaucer's original writings were illuminated with detailed illustrations. Early editions of Chaucer borrowed heavily from these elaborate illustrations found in manuscript copies. Today production costs and larger press runs make these illustrations too expensive, but historians still study the original artwork for additional clues about Chaucer and his life.

Chaucer was the first author to write at length in the English language. Most medieval writers would automatically have shaped their thoughts in Latin rather than their native tongue. Latin was considered to be the basic permanent language that would never change, while English was known to be a changing, fluid thing. The great authors had always written in Latin.

If Chaucer was not going to write in Latin, then we might have expected him to write in French instead. Most people spoke French, and it was thought to be a more "polite" or high-society language than English. Many of the other authors of Chaucer's day wrote in French when they were not writing in Latin. Chaucer was comfortable in both Latin and French. He had translated several Latin and French classic works into English, demonstrating his ease and familiarity with these languages.

George Macy wrote of *The Canterbury Tales* that "all of humanity moves through its pages." The tales themselves, he says, "are full of an inimitable humor, at once friendly and shrewd. The points are often made casually, often with bludgeon strokes, but they are always human and illuminating." Three hundred years after Chaucer's death, the poet Dryden named him "the father of English poetry." Chaucer has borne the title ever since.

BONITA M. COX

Geoffrey Chaucer: "[T]he firste fyndere of our faire language"

"As courtier, office holder, soldier, ambassador, legislator, burgher of London, Chaucer knew everybody that was worth knowing, high or low. It is hard to imagine a career so thoroughly adapted to fit him for the great task for which he came into the world[:].... that he should record the age, in its habit as it lived." (Kittredge, 6–7) In the process of that recording, he would become, in the words of his contemporary Thomas Hoccleve, "the firste fyndere of our faire language." (4978) Chaucer, however, set neither of these tasks for himself. His is not the voice of a chronicler; he wrote literature, not history. And in the beginning, although he wrote in English, that literature was French.

THE (RE)BIRTH OF ENGLISH LITERATURE

Throughout much of the fourteenth century, England was a cultural satellite of France. The Norman Conquest in 1066 had made French the official language of English government. Among the non-noble classes, whose members had no stake in government, English continued to be the oral standard in the following centuries, and by the end of the thirteenth century many of the Norman nobility had learned English for practical purposes. Still, at the time of Chaucer's birth "French was still the language of the royal court, of the Parliament, of lawyers and the law courts, of public records ... of schools, of letter writing when Latin wasn't used, and of town councils and guilds.... it was the international language of diplomacy and chivalry ... [and] ... the international language

37

of trade." (Howard, 22) Of the post-Conquest English kings, Edward III (1327–1377) is thought to be the first to speak English well, and his grandson and successor Richard II (1377–1399) was probably the first to speak it fluently. It is highly unlikely, however, that either wrote or read it; such records that exist indicate that neither kings' library contained any English texts. (Fisher, 83; Baugh & Cable, 142)

Chaucer must have been at least orally bilingual from childhood; he would have grown up speaking both French and English. By his early adolescence, when he began his training as a courtier and court diplomat, he would have been literately trilingual, reading and writing equally well in French, English, and Latin. Virtually every document with which he would have came into contact during his more than thirty years of combined royal and public service would have been written in either French or Latin. His wife's father was a native of France.

As the language of the French court, the model of chivalric society throughout all of Europe, French was also the language of most courtly literature. This was particularly the case in England, whose indigenous literary tradition, known to modern scholarship as Old English or Anglo-Saxon literature and exemplified by such works as *Beowulf* and "The Seafarer," had been lost in the onslaught of Norman French culture after the Conquest. Had such works even been available physically to an aspiring English poet, linguistically they would have been inaccessible; the English language had changed so much by the fourteenth century that Old English literature was no longer intelligible. Chaucer would undoubtedly have heard, and perhaps even read, some native verse, but most of it would have been modeled on French exemplars. For the young Chaucer, then, the very *idea* of literature would have been French. (Howard, 23)

Chaucer would have *thought* of literature as French, then, and he quite probably wrote some French verse during his early years as a courtier-in-training (Howard, 23, 506), but by the early 1360s—the probable date of composition of his earliest surviving poem, "ABC" (87–91)—he had obviously chosen to *write* literature in English. This choice can be explained by a combination of factors: the change in the status of the English language during Chaucer's lifetime; his audience; and the fact that writing was for him an avocation rather than a primary occupation.

While French and Latin remained the primary languages of fourteenth-century English "officialdom," by mid-century they were not its *only* language. The widespread Plague-depopulation beginning in 1348 increased the economic importance of both the laboring and the merchant classes, and thus the importance of the English language, which they spoke. (Baugh & Cable, 139–140) That same depopulation created a shortage of able, experienced teachers in proportion to the number of students that needed to be educated, which resulted in a shift away from traditional methods of doing things (or a general decline in the quality of education, depending on one's perspective); in most English grammar schools after 1349, "to save time and relieve the strain on teachers, or on some teachers' French" (Howard, 24), Latin was translated and parsed not in French but in English. (Baugh & Cable, 147) The status of the native tongue was further enhanced by the growing sense of English nationalism that followed the victories over the French at Crécy (1346) and Poitiers (1356), which were won not by Anglo-Norman knights but by English-speaking longbowmen. English was granted official status in London in 1356, when its mayor and aldermen ordered that proceedings in the sheriff's courts of London and Middlesex take place in English; six years later (in 1362), that status went national, when Parliament enacted the *Statute of Pleading*, which decreed that all lawsuits "be pleaded, shewed, defended, answered, debated, and judged in the English tongue, and that they be entered and enrolled in Latin". (Baugh & Cable, 145–146) If vernacular English was good enough for the schools, the courts, and the soldiers who made the nation proud, then it was certainly an acceptable medium for literature— especially for a literature that was largely spoken.

The audience for whom Chaucer wrote all of his work until the *Canterbury Tales* was quite small, members of a noble or royal household who would have experienced his work as listeners rather than as readers. There is abundant evidence to show that oral reading, before or after dinner, or by arranged invitation in honor of a special occasion, was commonplace in royal or noble households of the late Middle Ages. (Green, *Poets*, 97–100) Most nobles could read, but "Before the printing press, reading took more time and effort: every scribe's handwriting required an adjustment, there were numerous abbreviations, light was poor, eyeglasses inefficient" (Howard, 57); it was far easier, therefore, and much more pleasant, to listen. Chaucer's own idea of an "audience" would have been close to the word's etymological sense of "those within hearing," and his work was filled with references to those who "hear" or "harken" or to whom he is "telling" his "tale". (Strohm, 46) A beautiful copy of Chaucer's *Troilus and Criseyde*, made at some time in the first quarter of the fifteenth century, contains a frontspiece that depicts a middle-aged man addressing a royal court from a lectern in a garden. Because the speaker's face is very like other portraits of Chaucer, it is generally assumed that the speaker is Chaucer at the court of Richard II. Whether this is the intention cannot be proved, but the picture is important for what it says about the poet—"that a decade or two after his death Chaucer was still thought of as an oral poet, and his audience was still thought of as a court". (Howard, 347) Like all writers, Chaucer wanted an audience, and since there is also abundant evidence to show that by the early 1360s many nobles struggled with their French but most understood English (Baugh & Cable, 132–153), that was the best language to use to ensure that he had one.

Until 1391, when he resigned from his last "official" position, Chaucer was—as courtier, diplomat, world traveler, public administrator, and legislator, not to mention husband and father (of perhaps four children, though the record is not clear on that point)—a very busy man. Writing was something he would have done in his spare time, most probably at night, after a long day "on the job," and very likely in much the same state as that described by the comic eagle in *The House of Fame*:[1]

> For when thy labor doon al is,
> And hast maad alle thy rekeninges,
> In stede of rest and newe thinges,
> Thou goost hom to thy hous anoon,
> And, also domb as any stoon,
> Thou sittest at another book
> Til fully daswed is thy look....
>
>   (II. 144–150)

Under such circumstances, writing in one's native tongue would be the obvious choice.

CHAUCER'S ENGLISH

Which brings us to the nature of that native tongue: as is clear from the above passage, Chaucer's English is different from our own. That difference, however, is mostly a matter of spelling and vocabulary.

Though French had become England's "official" language after the Norman Conquest, English continued to be the language of the non-noble classes. Because it had no "official" status, however, it also had no standard form. One of the most striking characteristics of the language of Chaucer's time—known to us as Middle English, to mark its period in the language's 1,500-year evolution—is its great diversity. Dialects differed not only from county to county but often even among areas within a county. As late as the first half of the fifteenth century, the author of *The Myroure of Oure Ladye* commented that "Our language is also so dyverse in yt selfe, that the commen maner of spekyng in Englysshe of some contre [county] can skante be understonded in some other contre of the same londe". (Baugh & Cable, 184) As people spoke, so did they write, representing sounds in characters as best they could. But representations of a single sound could be achieved through numerous symbols; for example, the characters ∂ and ? represented the two different *th* sounds, as in *wi∂* (*with*) and *?an* (*then*). With this combine the regional differences in the sounds of words, and the often extreme idiosyncrasies of individual scribes, to make a Middle English spelling system that is eccentric at best.

Beyond the foreignness of Chaucer's spelling, however, his English is not all that different from the literary English of any later period. Chaucer's works, like those of Shakespeare, Milton, Wordsworth, and countless other poets, include words that are no longer used, or otherwise non-standard, and words that are in current use but whose meanings have changed over time. They also contain a few idiomatic expressions unique to Middle English, and a few inflectional survivals from Old English that have now disappeared; all these words and expressions are glossed in modern editions. Chaucer's vocabulary and grammar therefore present no great obstacle for a modern reader. Excepting occasional shifts—ever the prerogative of the poet, the very foundation of "poetic license"—Chaucer's syntax is essentially the same as our own. Thus, while it may appear odd or difficult *prima faciae*, Chaucer's work is really quite accessible to the modern reader.

Chaucer was himself very aware of the problems presented by so many varying forms of English during his time. He comments openly about this problem toward the end of *Troilus and Criseyde*:

And for there is so great diversite
In Englissh and in writyng of oure tongue,

So prey I God that non miswrite the
Ne the mysmetre for defaute of tonge.

(V. 1793–96)

But Chaucer's understanding of the problems of literature as text surpassed orthography; as is clear in his seven-line poem "Chaucers Wordes Unto Adam, His Owne Scrivener" ("Geffrey unto Adame His Owen Scryvene"), he was also well acquainted with unreliable scribes. His chastisement of Adam speaks to any writer whose work has passed through another's hands:

Adam scriveyn, if ever it thee bifalle
Boece or Troylus for to wryten newe,
Under thy long lokkes thou most have the scalle,
But after my makyng thow wryte more trewe;
So ofte adaye I mot thy werk renewe,
It to correcte and eke to rubbe and scrape,
And al is thorugh thy negligence and rape.

Chaucer knew that language changed over time, and he seems even to have anticipated that the time would come when his readers might struggle. He states in the prologue to Book II of *Troilus and Criseyde* that

Ye know eke that in forme of speeche is chaunge
Withinne a thousand yeer, and wordes tho
That hadden pris, now wonder nyce and straunge
Us thinketh hem, and yet thei spake hem so,
And spedde as well in love as men now do....

(II. 22–26)

But he earnestly hoped that his words, however quaint or strange his future readers might find them, would not be lost. "Go, little book," he says of *Troilus and Criseyde*, "and wherever you are read or sung, I beseech God that you will be understood." (V. 1786, 1796–98)

Chaucer's native dialect was that of metropolitan London, where he was born and educated and lived most of his life. His usage, however, was necessarily influenced by that of the court for which he wrote and, to some extent, that of literary tradition. This was more conservative and contained a greater number of characteristics peculiar to the speech of

Southern England than did the ordinary speech of the city, which was the dialect from which a national standard would evolve in the century following his death. (Baugh & Cable, 189) When Hoccleve refers to Chaucer as "the firste fyndere of our faire language" (4978), then, he does not mean that Chaucer's was the dialect from which Standard English derived. He means that Chaucer was the first to use English in a way that was "fair" in an aesthetic sense. Chaucer is an important figure in the history and development of the English *language*, but he is still more important in the history and development of English *literature.* In that sphere, Chaucer was no conservative: "He was a great innovator" who "showed that English could be written with an elegance and power that earlier writers had not attained". (Benson, xxx)

CHAUCER'S LITERARY CAREER: AN OVERVIEW

Scholars generally distinguish three phases of Chaucer's literary career: his French period (before 1373), during which he was so completely under the control of French literary traditions that he was essentially a French poet writing in English; his Italian period (1373–1387), during which he was inspired by Italian writers and broadened the scope of his work through copious reading; and his English period (1388–1400), during which he applied his knowledge to the representation of English life and the English character. Though convenient, such classification in periods is misleading, for it suggests that there are obvious and significant differences between the literary accomplishments of Chaucer's early periods and those of his last and that these differences are the result of a readily discernible evolution. While this may be true of many writers, it is not necessarily the case with Chaucer. Because "he was the most restlessly experimental of poets, constantly trying and mastering, then abandoning but sometimes later returning to genres, metrical forms, styles, and subject matter" (Benson, xxix), and because his literary accomplishments are so varied, much of Chaucer's work defies categorization, chronological or otherwise.

His first and last major works, *The Book of the Duchess* and *The Canterbury Tales*, differ considerably—the former is an elegy cast in the form of a dream and the latter a collection of stories assembled within the framework of a pilgrimage—but the two share the premise of narration from experience. *The House of Fame*, written during his middle or Italian period, proceeds from the same idea, except that its narrator/persona, whom the eagle calls "Geffrey" (729), is clearly identified as Chaucer himself. The five-stress decasyllabic line, the iambic pentameter, that would become the standard of later English poetry, and which Chaucer uses in most of *The Canterbury Tales*, appears also in the work of his earlier career: in the "ABC," probably the earliest of his surviving poems, and in *The Legend of Good Women*, begun during the Italian period and revised during the English period. *Troilus and Criseyde* and *The Parliament of Fowls* of the Italian period are both written in seven-line "rhyme royal"; so, too, are four of the *Canterbury Tales*. "The Life of Saint Cecile" and the story of Palamon and Arcite date to the early Italian period, but Chaucer inserted revisions of these into *The Canterbury Tales* of his English period as the tales of the Knight and the Second Nun. The same is true of "The Monk's Tale," a work of the 1370s to which Chaucer added the "modern instances" of four contemporary tragedies during the English period. The *Canterbury Tales* are themselves so varied that they constitute "a veritable anthology of medieval literature" (Baugh, 152): romance, parody, allegory, *fabliau*, Breton *lai*, beast fable, saint's life, *exemplum*, miracle of the Virgin, satire, literary confession, sermon, moral treatise, classical legend, tragedy and comedy, pathos and irony, dialogue and monologue—and the work isn't even complete.

Both early and late in his career, Chaucer wrote prose. His translation of Boethius' *De Consolatione philosophiae* (*The Consolation of Philosophy*) and of Renaud de Louens' *Le Livre de Melibée et de Dame Prudence*, a French version of Albertanus of Brescia's *Liber de consolationis et consilii* (*Book of Consolation and Counsel*) were both written midway through the Italian period, very probably with the young Richard II as their intended audience. (Howard, 383) The Boethius translation survived on its own as *Boece*, but "The Tale of Melibee" became in his English period one of the two *Tales* told by Chaucer himself. His two other prose pieces, "The Parson's Tale," with which *The Canterbury Tales* concludes, and his *Treatise on the Astrolabe*, which is addressed to "little Louis my son," belong clearly to his English period. The *Treatise on the Astrolabe* is the first user manual written in English (and one of the clearest!), which grants Chaucer the additional distinction of being our first Technical Writer.

And then, of course, there are the lost works. Chaucer mentions two of them in the early version of the prologue to *The Legend of Good*

Women (version F, written most probably in 1386) and a third in a revised version of the same text (version G, written after 1394). The first two could belong to either his French or his Italian period, and the last to any of the three. He mentions several others in his "Retraction" to *The Canterbury Tales*. Certainly written quite late in his life, the "Retraction" contains what is clearly intended to be a summary of his literary accomplishments; the works listed there that have not survived, therefore, could belong, in part or whole, to any of his three periods. We have no way of knowing.

What we *do* know is that throughout his career, as he was creating new works he was also revising and adapting his earlier work to suit new purposes and audiences. He may indeed have been "endowed at birth with the splendid accident of genius" (Kittredge, 30), but he was also a practical poet who took great care never to offend a patron—past, present, or potential. Though he clearly took his writing quite seriously and addressed in it most of the important social, political, religious, and literary issues of his time, he seems to have obscured his own ideas. We rarely see what Chaucer-the-man thinks, and we are more often than not unsure of exactly what he means. He entertains, he informs, he instructs, and he makes us laugh—but in the final analysis he remains mysterious.

THE BOOK OF THE DUCHESS: A CONSOLATION

The Book of the Duchess is Chaucer's earliest datable poem. It is what is known as an "occasional poem," written to commemorate the death of John of Gaunt's first wife, Blanche, the Duchess of Lancaster, who died of the Plague in September, 1368. Chaucer and the Lancasters were close in age and had known each other for some years, so it was natural that he would have wanted to express his grief by praising Blanche and offering sympathy and consolation to Gaunt. Chaucer most probably began the poem soon after Blanche's death, certainly by early 1369; and he would have finished at least a fairly complete first draft of it no later than 1371, when Kathryn Swynford, Chaucer's sister-in-law, replaced Blanch in Gaunt's bed as his mistress. We may assume that this was not Chaucer's first poem, since it shows him to be already quite skilled in the idiom and conventions of love poetry. It would nevertheless have been a major undertaking for the young poet. However friendly the Lancasters and the Chaucers may have been, Gaunt was, after all, a son of Edward III and one of England's richest and most powerful barons; he was therefore not someone a ambitious young poet could afford to offend. Those circumstances may account for the poem's odd mix of convention and eccentricity.

The poem's basic form is that of an elegy cast as a dream vision: the dreamer, who just happens to also be a poet, falls asleep after reading Ovid's tragic story of Ceys and Alcyone. He dreams that he is in a wood, where the emperor "Octovien" is leading a hunt, and where, following a small dog, he comes upon an obviously grief-stricken, black-clad knight, who, when asked about the source of his sorrow, tells the dreamer that he has played a game of chess with Fortune and lost his queen. The obtusely literal dreamer misses the metaphor, so the knight tells his story: how he met and fell in love with a lady named White, whom he describes in detail—praising her beauty, her accomplishments, her gentleness, her goodness; how he won her heart; and how they lived together in perfect harmony for many years. At this point, the dreamer interrupts, asking "Where is she now?" Stunned and clearly frustrated by the dreamer's simplemindedness, the knight replies that her loss is what he's been talking about, and that he's lost more than the dreamer could possibly understand. Still missing the point, the dreamer asks, "Alas, sir how? What might that be?" Forced thus by the dreamer's dim wit to speak the yet unspeakable plain truth, the knight finally does: "She is dead!" The dreamer's response, "By God, it's a pity," is just as plain. With that, the horn sounds, ending the hunt, and the knight rides homeward. The dreamer awakens and decides to write a poem about his "curious" dream.

In many respects, *The Book of the Duchess* is conventional and unoriginal. Its basic storyline, its befuddled dreamer, and several of its specifics, including in some cases actual lines, come directly from Chaucer's French models, the works of Froissart, Machaut, and Deschamps. None of these sources, however, is a true elegy, which makes Chaucer's appropriation of them for this purpose an original one. As Donaldson notes, Chaucer's dreamer-poet is "at times almost too stupid to be true." Humor is not something one expects in an elegy. Yet it is precisely the dreamer's humorous stupidity that forces the knight to complete the grieving process: to accept the loss as a part of life and to move on. (1116) The horn that ends the hunt and sends the knight back to his "long castle with white walls / By Saint John, on a rich hill"

(1318–19) serves as a wake-up call to both the knight and the dreamer-poet. Via the wordplay here that refers specifically to John of Gaunt, who was both Duke of Lancaster ("long castle") and Earl of Richmond ("rich hill"), Gaunt is called home, back into the world, with his memories of the fair Blanche intact (white walls) and a future still to live for; now free from his paralyzing grief, the "hart-hunting" for this knight is "all done." The same is true for the dreamer-poet, who is called now to turn his dream into a poem, which he ends with "now it is done."

THE CURIOUS *HOUSE OF FAME*

Chaucer's most controversial poem, certainly, is the unfinished *The House of Fame*—about which critics seem to agree on very little except that it is eclectic, elusive, and in parts absolutely delightful. Like *The Book of the Duchess*, which predates it by probably ten or so years, *The House of Fame* is a dream vision occasioned by the reading of a book, Virgil's *Aeneid*. The dreamer-poet here, however, is named "Geffrey," which suggests that the dream is to be read as Chaucer's own. After a prologue that seems to mock epic conventions, the poet tells us that on a December night he dreamed he was in a temple of Venus, on the glass walls of which was depicted the story of *The Aeneid*, which he reads and retells with an emphasis on the story of Aeneas and Dido. He then steps outside, where he sees a huge golden eagle flying toward him. In Book II, the eagle seizes him and they soar aloft; as the frightened Chaucer dangles helplessly from the eagle's claws, the eagle explains: he has been sent by Jove to rescue the poet from his hermit-like existence in the world of books, where he's become too removed from what's happening in the world around him, and take him to the House of Fame, where he will hear abundant tidings of "Love's folk" as a reward for his long service to Venus and Cupid. Book II then relates their airborne journey, the account of which—with its contrast between the eagle's friendly chatter and the poet's speechless terror—is one of the finest comic episodes in all of literature.

In Book III, the dreamer-poet and the eagle arrive at the Temple of Fame, where the Goddess receives petitioners who come seeking positive reputations in literary history. What Chaucer learns is that the Goddess is willful and arbitrary: some who deserve fame are granted it; others who are equally deserving are granted ill fame; others of the deserving are consigned to oblivion; and some who actually deserve ill fame are granted just the opposite. After observing Fame's capricious judgments for some time, the poet is asked by a stranger if he is there to seek fame. His response is slightly petulant: No, he says, I'm not after fame; in fact, I'd be perfectly satisfied if people would just leave my name alone. I know best how I stand. (1873–1882) He is then led by the eagle and the stranger to the House of Rumor, which is an elongated wicker structure that whirls continuously. Inside it is a great congregation of people exchanging bits and pieces of gossip that take physical shape, as rumors, and fly out of this structure to the House of Fame, where the Goddess names them, assigns them lifespans, and sends them down to earth. Because the rumors must compete for priority when leaving the wicker structure, true and false rumors sometimes join forces and become a single entity. As the poet watches these odd happenings, his observations are suddenly interrupted by the arrival of a man "of great authority," who is about to make an announcement. On that note, the poem ends.

Because this announcement could well tie this poem's varied content and elusive structure together, it has been the subject of much critical speculation. Is the man of authority there to bring important "tydyinges" that have to do with "Love's folke"? If so, that might mean that the poem is to be taken as an "occasion" piece, written to celebrate one or another of the various royal betrothals that were being considered or were under negotiation at the time of the poem's composition. Or, as may be suggested by the opening references to the *Aeneid* and such borrowings from Dante as the marvelous mid-life journey (at age 37 in 1379, Chaucer would certainly have considered himself midway through his own life's journey), the supernatural guide (the golden eagle could easily be read as the Roman standard and thus a Virgil stand-in), and the three-book structure, might the man be there to say something important about literature, about a poet's responsibility or the sources of his knowledge? There is, after all, a great deal said in this poem about books, authority, knowledge, experience, and poetic vision. Alas, we'll never know. Donaldson may well be right when he says that Chaucer abandoned the poem "because it got out of hand." (1117) It is a handful, yes, both flawed and peculiar; but it is nevertheless also a wonderfully provocative read.

THE PARLIAMENT OF FOWLS AND
CHAUCER'S SATIRICAL VOICE

This poem is very possibly the first celebration of St Valentine's Day ever written. It is yet another of his dream visions, with a narrator whose dream is occasioned by what he is reading; this time it is Cicero's *Dream of Scipio*. The narrator, who is a student of love (he reads about it) but yearns to be one of its practitioners, dreams that the Africanus of Scipio's dream appears to him, promises to show him "matter to write," and leads him into Venus' garden of romantic love. There he finds the Goddess Nature presiding over a great flock of birds that are gathered for their annual choosing of mates. The birds are presented in a social hierarchy: birds of prey are the highest, followed in order of rank by those birds who eat worms, those who live on the water, and those who eat seeds. Each is there to chose its mate. As the highest in rank, the eagles (the "Tercels") are to choose first, but their choosing is impeded by a dispute among three male eagles who all want the same beautiful female (the "Formel"). Each of the Tercels—one royal, the other two noble, but not royal—states his case and a debate ensues in which intensity of devotion is set against length of devotion. When the ordinary birds grow impatient at having to wait for their own mating and begin interrupting the Tercels' debate with rude comments, Nature intercedes and organizes them all into a "parliament" charged with determining which of the three Tercels the Formel should choose, with one speaker representing each of the four groups of birds. Their arguments represent both upper- and lower-class attitudes and speech, and, like many sessions of the English Parliament during that era (and indeed in our own), it soon degenerates into a shouting match. Once again, Nature steps in, declaring that, if she were Reason, she would advise the Formel to choose the royal Tercel. (631–33) She is not Reason, however; she is Nature, so the birds must make their own choices. The Formel asks then to be allowed a year to make her decision; Nature and the three Tercels agree. The rest of the birds then choose their mates by mutual agreement, sing a song in honor of St Valentine, and fly away as happy couples. The noise they make as they depart wakes the narrator, who returns to his books, still looking to find what he wants but does not have.

As is characteristic of so much of Chaucer's poetry, *The Parliament of Fowls* is a wonderful mixture of humor and seriousness, made possible here to a great extent by his choice to write it in "rhyme royal" (a five-stress line in seven-line stanzas), which was flexible enough to accommodate the poem's different levels of language—the smooth elegance of the passages describing Venus' Temple (which he borrows almost whole from Boccaccio's *Teseida*), the stately courtliness of the aristocratic eagles' speech, and the colloquial cheekiness of the birds of the "lowere kynde," including some actual "bird talk," such as "Kek Kek! Cuckoo! Quack, quack!" (449); this use of language to depict social class and attitudes anticipates what he will later do on a far larger scale in *The Canterbury Tales*. On the one hand, *The Parliament of Fowls* is a humorous poem that good-naturedly satirizes Parliamentary government and class distinctions, which a courtly audience would certainly have enjoyed. On the other, it is a philosophical poem that surveys love, both human and divine, in all its various forms. It is also a poem that makes an important political point: royal marriages are different from ordinary ones; they are political alliances that can affect an entire kingdom and should not be entered into without due diligence and careful consideration on both sides.

TROILUS AND CRISEYDE

Of his finished works, *Troilus and Criseyde* is considered Chaucer's greatest literary achievement. Its 8239 lines in rhyme royal are a retelling of Bocaccio's *Filostrato*, a copy of which Chaucer very probably acquired during his second trip to Italy, in 1378. From Boccaccio, Chaucer takes the plot, the principal characters, and the sequence of events: During the Trojan war, Troilus, a son of Priam, the Trojan king, falls in love with Criseyde, a beautiful young woman whose traitorous father, Calchas, has gone over to the Greek side. With the help of Criseyde's uncle, Pandarus, Troilus courts and eventually wins Criseyde as his mistress, and for three years the two of them share a mutual love that is perfect in all ways. They are forced to part when an exchange of prisoners requires that Criseyde join her father in the Greek camp. Swearing undying love and fidelity for Troilus, Criseyde leaves Troy, but she promises to find a way to return within ten days. By the time those ten days have passed, however, she has transferred her affections to her Greek escort, Diomede, and within only a few months she has given him the brooch that had been Troilus' parting gift to her. Troilus is devastated by her betrayal and is eventually killed in battle by Achilles.

For the modern reader, such "borrowing," particularly since Chaucer nowhere mentions either Boccaccio or the *Filostrato*, would be a clear case of plagiarism. That would not, however, have been the case for a medieval reader, whose ideas of originality differ radically from the current:

> Originality was not one of the primary virtues expected of poets in the Middle Ages. In narrative poetry the authenticity of the story was a better guarantee of audience-appeal. In an age when the conditions of publication had not yet created the concept of property rights in ideas, and the word *plagiarism* did not exist in any language, all literary material was in the public domain and poets took their stories wherever they found them. In deciding to retell Boccaccio's story in English, Chaucer was doing something entirely normal. (Baugh, 75)
>
> For all that it owes a great deal to Bocccaccio (including some 2750 lines that Chaucer translates whole into his poem, as they suit his purposes), *Troilus and Criseyde* is nevertheless an "original" in the sense that its tone and characterization are significantly different from those of the *Filostrato*. Chaucer's characters are far more developed and complex than Boccaccio's, and his approach to their revelation is more psychological, emphasizing motives and mental states far more than action and events. (75, 81)

Those motives and mental states reflect the values of a culture so drastically different from our own, however, that modern readers often have difficulty in even understanding them. Chaucer's *Troilus and Criseyde* belongs to a world in which lovers played the game of courtly love, the rules of which were codified in a twelfth-century book, *De Amore,* by Andreas Capellanus. Because marriages among the upper-class in the Middle Ages rarely considered the sentiments of the parties involved, extramarital attachment was not uncommon. The doctrine of courtly love provided a code of conduct for activities of this sort. The code included the following: Because marriage is not a lover's goal, both married and unmarried lovers can play, and because love between a husband and wife is impossible, marriage cannot be used as an excuse for refusing to take a lover. For the male lover, the following applies: he can experience true love for only *one* woman; he must worship her at first from afar; he must fear that he may never be accepted or prove worthy; though he may have a single confidant, he must generally suffer secretly; he should tremble and turn pale in her presence, suffer sleeplessness, and lose his appetite; and if and when the woman accepts him, he must conduct his affair with great discretion in order to protect the lady's reputation. For the female lover, the following applies: she should be hard to win, or she should appear to be; she may be capricious and seemingly heartless, but in the end she should give her favors willingly; she must guard her reputation and conduct her affair in secret, although she too may have a single confidante. For both, absolute fidelity is crucial.

By Chaucer's day, the conventions of courtly love had become mostly literary, and they formed the lens through which his audience would have viewed *Troilus and Criseyde*. (Baugh, 79; Shoaf, xxi–xxv) It is important to remember also that while the story of Troilus and Criseyde is set in Troy, its audience is an English courtly society that at the time of the poem's composition was dominated by the values of an adolescent king, Richard II, for whom idealized romantic love and extravagant bravery would have had great appeal.

In such a context, Troilus is the perfect courtly lover: young, inexperienced, and idealistic. We see him first with his young knights, looking at the ladies and mocking lovers. And then we see him struck by Cupid's arrow—love at first sight. Afraid of rejection, he indulges in typical adolescent behavior: he sighs, he weeps, he swoons; he grows pale and cannot eat. His is adolescent angst at its best, and worst. Though he is counted as one of Troy's greatest warriors (second only to his brother, Hector), in matters of love he is timid and fearful. He relies absolutely and entirely on his older and wiser friend, Criseyde's uncle Pandarus, to script the plan that will "fix him up with the girl of his dreams." After he wins her and they become lovers, he believes absolutely in the "happily-ever-after" scenario of first love, young love, as very probably did Richard II when he married Anne of Bohemia at age 15 (she was 16). Troilus' behavior following Crisedye's betrayal may seem extravagantly emotional to the modern reader, but it is no more so than king Richard's reaction to Queen Anne's death in 1394, when he "raged tempestuously and had their favorite palace at Sheen destroyed." And Richard was then no adolescent, but a man in his full prime, 27 years old. (Brewer, 202) For Chaucer's audience and according to the conventions of the "game" of courtly love, then, Troilus is a model prince.

As is Pandarus a model friend. Troilus needs his help, and Pandarus devotes himself entirely to making his friend happy, whatever it takes. And if it takes making his niece a royal mistress, that was not necessarily a bad thing in fourteenth-century England. Chaucer's own sister-in-law was, after all, John of Gaunt's mistress. As Troilus is an idealist, Pandarus is a realist: a young widow could do worse for herself than enjoy the love and protection of a prince of the realm. That he derives vicarious enjoyment from orchestrating the love affair between Troilus and his niece should not be held against him. By medieval standards, he was looking out for both their interests. Why should that not give one satisfaction?

By those same rules and standards, however, Criseyde is set up as the "faithless woman." And it is very clearly a "set-up." That she should be condemned for a lack of faithfulness by a code that exists solely for the very purpose of facilitating unfaithfulness is the most ironic of ironies. Of the poem's three courtly love players, Criseyde's motives and mental states are the least easiest to grasp because her characterization exemplifies that aspect of Chaucer's style that has intrigued his readers for more than 600 years: his indeterminacy, his ambiguity, what Donaldson calls his "elusion of clarity ... by which he evades, for the sake of poetic complexity, the laws and obligations of logical simplicity". ("Elusion," 23)

Criseyde is introduced in the poem after an account of her father's treachery, which concludes with the statement that the Trojan people believed the traitor and all his family should be executed, "burned, skin and bones." (I, 90–91) On that note, we first hear of his daughter, who, though uninvolved in any way in Calchas' treason, "fears for her life." She is described as an angelically beautiful young widow, "friendless and alone"; she is so frightened and alone that "nearly out of her mind for sorrow and fear.... with pitious vice and tenderly weeping," she appeals to Hector for protection. (92–112) When Troilus first sees her at the feast in the temple, she is "completely ... and silently alone"; she stands apart from the rest of the gathering, "near the door," as if she might need to flee for her life at any moment. (176–180) She is, as Donaldson puts it, "a damsel in distress if there ever was one." ("Elusion," 29) When Pandarus visits her to press Troilus' suit, however, we see a very different Criseyde. This one is a woman of independent means sufficient enough to afford her a large and convivial household with several servants and ladies-in-waiting, and at least two nieces. And then, of course, there is uncle Pandarus himself, a man we're later told is an important enough person in Troy to spend the whole day with the king (V, 281–5), and who is Prince Troilus' best friend; from their affectionate greetings and amiable conversation, it's clear that uncle and niece have a long-standing relationship as good friends. (II, 78–93) This Criseyde is no damsel in distress. She is neither friendless nor alone. She is not struck by Cupid's arrow; nor is she tricked or manipulated into becoming Troilus' lover. Hers is a reasoned decision, and she sets the rules of their relationship: he defers to her in all things. For three years, her affection for Troilus is as constant as his is for her. She is a clever, charming, confident woman, fully in control of her life.

And then she isn't. She's to be sent from Troy in exchange for Antenor (who will himself prove to be a traitor). She's distraught. She's confident. She has a plan. She loves Troilus, and she will return. In the Greek camp, however, where there were few women, she becomes again the damsel in distress. If she is caught escaping, she will be considered a spy; she knows from Troy what happens to spies. What she fears most, though, is "falling into the hands of some wretch, after which she might as well be dead." (V, 701–706) Once again, then, fearing for her life, she is "alone and in need of a friend's help." (1025–26) The poet/narrator says Crisedye is "slydying of corage" (825), which is generally glossed as meaning something like "unstable of heart," "changeable of determination," or "wavering of temperament." Set as it is in that part of the text that describes her situation just after Diomede has fastened on his plan to "bring Criseyde's heart into his net" (771–77), however, "slydyng of corage" might just as easily be glossed as "vulnerable," which, at that point, she certainly is. The poet follows that line with an odd comment, that he cannot tell her age. (826) Does her age somehow come into play here? Does it connect meaningfully in some way with the description of Troilus in the next stanza as a "young lion"? (830) Probably, but Chaucer leaves that connection to the reader to find and interpret. Criseyde praises Troilus' "constancy" (1056–57), yet she chooses the "sodeyn" [impetuous] Diomede. (1024) She honestly regrets hurting Troilus and hopes God will send him happiness in reward for his gentleness and worthiness, which she values highly. (1056–57) Yet, in her only response to his several "pitiful" letters pleading with her to keep her promise, she accuses him of thinking only of his own pleasure and leading her on with false expectations. (1607–15) While her decision to take Diomede as her lover may make sense for several reasons, her motives for sending Troilus such a letter are enigmatic, as are Chaucer's; the letter is one of his "original" additions to the Boccaccio text.

Where does Chaucer stand on Criseyde? On the one hand he says that, because she suffered so as the result of her betrayal, he would forgive her if he could. (1095–99) On the other, he apologizes to the ladies in his audience for telling a story that casts women in such a bad light. (1772–75) Chaucer likes to have it both ways. In Book I, for instance, we have "sely Troilus" (871); in Book V, Criseyde is a "sely woman." (1095) The word "sely" can be glossed with several meanings. It means "innocent," "blessed," "ignorant," and "foolish"; it also means "hapless" and "wretched." Which is it in which place? Such ambiguity is typical of Chaucer.

THE CONSOLATION OF PHILOSOPHY AND THE LEGEND OF GOOD WOMEN

At the same time that he was making "original" use of the Italian *Filostrato* for his English *Troilus and Criseyde*, Chaucer was also translating the Latin text of Boethius' *Consolation of Philosophy* and the French text of Renaud de Louens' *Le Livre de Melibée et de Dame Prudence* (a condensation of a thirteenth-century Latin work) into English prose. Both works address topics useful for a ruler and were very probably written to be read by the young Richard II as part of his education. Both are faithful translations, except for a passage in the *Melibee* that deals with the dangers of having a boy king, which Chaucer tactfully omits. (Howard, 383) Boethius "is a book about the order of things, about power, about the place of randomness in the governance of a society.... It was essential reading for a monarch." (379) King Alfred and Queen Elizabeth I both translated it into English for their own use. The *Melibee* discusses "some of the imponderables that those of the ruling class must face: how to choose advisors, whose advice to take or ignore, when to declare war.... and how to [negotiate] a just peace." (383) Though there was a recognizable kind of artful prose that was used in sermons, letters, and certain kinds of moral treatises, there was in Chaucer's time no tradition of literary prose as we know it (380), and neither of these works does anything to alter that situation. They do, however, demonstrate Chaucer's interest in and facility with languages other than English. As noted above, the Boethius survives on its own as *Boece*, and the *Melibee* becomes one of the tales Chaucer himself tells in *The Canterbury Tales*.

That *Troilus and Criseyde* attracted the attention of the ladies to whom he apologizes at its end is made clear in the prologue to *The Legend of Good Women*, in which Cupid, the God of Love, takes Chaucer to task for writing works (such as the story of Criseyde) that portray women as distrustful and thus turn people against love. With Cupid is a great queen, named Alceste, who comes to the poet's defense, citing those of his works that have served women and love well. Though its tone is light hearted and humorous (and gratuitously self-promoting on Chaucer's part), the prologue makes it quite clear that *Troilus and Criseyde*, most particularly in its depiction of Criseyde, created quite a stir in court circles, the result of which seems to have been a number of heated discussions about the nature of women, discussions that of course continue still, in literature and in life. As penance for his offense, the prologue tells us that the poet is ordered to write a "glorious legend" in the form of a collection of stories about women who were faithful in love and the men who betrayed them. He will do this "year by year" for as long as he lives (481), beginning with the legend of Cleopatra and ending with that of Alceste. Because the ballade "Hide Absolon" mentions nineteen ladies (249) and the number nineteen is stated again later (283), we may assume that he originally intended to write nineteen stories. He wrote only nine, however, and the last is unfinished. Why? Howard's theory here makes sense: If "year by year" means that he was to write one legend a year; and if, as is generally accepted, the *Prologue* and the Cleopatra legend were written in 1386, followed by one legend each year until the death in 1394 of Queen Anne—generally assumed to be the model for the Queen Alceste of the poem—and the poet's consequent liberation from completeing his commission, then the total would be nine. The ninth legend, of Hypermnestra, is not quite finished; this suggests that Chaucer had tired of the enterprise and was happy to abandon it for another project he had been also working on at least since 1388. This replacement project, of course, was *The Canterbury Tales*. (395–96)

The nine stories that constitute the unfinished *Legend of Good Women* are very alike, almost formulaically so. Though they necessarily differ in details and particulars, each is, in essence, a retelling of *Troilus and Criseyde*, a story of true love, but with the roles reversed; the woman is betrayed by her male lover. By comparison to Chaucer's treatment of similar themes elsewhere, they are, as Brewer says, somewhat "thin." (255) The poem's *Prologue*, however, is one of Chaucer's most delightful works, a charming mix of old and new: its content is much like his early dream visions, but its verse is the iambic pentameter rhyming couplet that makes Chaucer the "inventor of English 'heroic verse'." (Howard, 265) The *Prologue* is also one of the most interesting of Chaucer's poems from the standpoint of what it tells us about his own motives and mental states during two very distinctly different periods in his life and poetic career.

The prologue to the *Legend of Good Women* exists in two forms, designated "F" and "G" versions according to the manuscripts in which they appear. Scholars generally agree that the F version is the earlier or 1386 original version. The F version contains a dedication of sorts to Queen Anne in Queen Alceste's instruction to the poem: "And when this book is made, give it to the queen/On my behalf, at Eltham or at Sheene." (496–97) Eltham and Sheen were the two favorite royal residences of Richard II and Queen Anne; Richard was so grief stricken on Anne's death in 1394 that he ordered Sheen to be destroyed. (Baugh, 213; Brewer, 247) The later G version, which dates to after the queen's death, omits this reference. Most of the G version revisions are clearly intended to improve the sense and quality of the poetry by clarifying some points and consolidating others; the G version eliminates much of the rambling of the earlier F version, the result of which is a tighter, more cohesive, and better organized poem. These revisions are interesting because of what they tell us about Chaucer the poet at work.

One revision, however, is important because of what it tells us about Chaucer the man. Both versions address at some length the proper conduct of a lord or a king, most of which is standard Aristotelian advice, "the sentence of the philosopher" (F, 381; G, 365): he should not be a tyrant; he should dispense justice equally to rich and poor alike; he should be compassionate and merciful; he should be loyal to those who serve him well and reward them appropriately, and so on. As part of that discussion in the earlier F version, the poet says that a king's subjects "are his treasure and the gold in his coffer" (380), which is an appropriate sentiment for a man who had been a customs officer, as Chaucer had been for some twelve years. The later G version replaces this line with six that say that it is a king's "deeply sworn duty" to show his people the simple kindness of hearing well their complaints and petitions in a timely manner. (360–66) This is a clear condemnation of King Richards's irresponsible behavior and autocratic attitude in the years following his official majority at the age of 22 and his claiming the right to govern on his own, without "protectors," in 1389.

The Lack of Political Steadfastness

Personal feuds and factional intrigues are commonplace in any royal court. When that court is presided over by a boy-king but actually ruled by a group of "protectors," however, court politics can and do create significant problems. In Richard II's court, though they were complicated by multiple and often shifting loyalties, there were basically three court parties vying for power and control: the King's party, made up of Richard and his closest friends; the opposition party, headed by the King's youngest uncle, the Earl of Gloucester; and the Lancastrian party, headed by John of Gaunt. Richard's party deeply resented the other two because they were keeping him from ruling in his own right. Gloucester, who had little wealth or power of his own, resented the other two because they were "haves" and he was (by comparison) a "have not"; because Gloucester did not dare to challenge his powerful brother Gaunt openly, however, he focused his malevolence on his nephew, the King. It fell to John of Gaunt, who was already indisputably the most powerful man in England, to maintain peace between the other two parties, which he managed to do for several years.

In 1386, however, Gaunt left for Castile to pursue his claim (through his wife, Constanza) to that throne. In his absence, the tensions between the other two parties escalated into open opposition. The king thumbed his nose at Gloucester and the "protectors" by indulging his favorites with financial and political plums that were, in the view of the opposition party, at best inappropriate and at worst illegal. Gloucester couldn't attack the king personally, however, so he went after his advisors. In the Parliament of 1386, of which Chaucer was an elected member, Gloucester demanded that both Richard's treasurer, John Fordham, and his chancellor, Michael de la Pole, be dismissed. Richard refused to comply and then refused even to attend Parliament itself. He then made the situation worse by making his friend Robert de Vere the duke of Ireland, a position Gloucester wanted for himself. When Gloucester initiated Parliamentary impeachment proceedings against Fordham and de la Pole, however, Richard had no choice but to appear in their defense.

There, the King's party lost. Fordham was dismissed; de la Pole was impeached, fined, and imprisoned; and Richard was forced accept members from Gloucester's party as their replacements. Richard was humiliated. When Parliament was dissolved, however, Richard remitted de la Pole's fines and converted his imprisonment to house arrest at Winchester Castle; he then held his Christmas court at Windsor, with de la Pole as his honored guest. This was to be Richard's only victory, though, because at that same Parliament Gloucester also established a Commission of Government, which took charge of the King's possessions and had the right to enter his properties at will. (Howard, 387–88) As an elected member of that Parliament, Chaucer would have witnessed all of this personally, and as a close friend of John of Gaunt he must have been intimately interested in the proceedings. Howard seems certain that the poem "Lack of Steadfastnesse" was written during these hard times (388), the first stanza of which may reflect Chaucer's feelings during that session:

> Some time the world was so steadfast and stable
> That mannes word was obligation;
> And now it is so false and deceivable
> That word and deed, as in conclusion,
> Is nothing like. For turnèd up-so-down
> Is all this world for meed and willfulnesse,
> That all is lost for lack of steadfastnesse.
>
> (1–7)

The sentiments of the poem echo a larger theme in Chaucer's life in this period. Between 1387 and 1389, Gloucester's party and his Commission of Government systematically removed virtually all the King's supporters from their positions, high or low—some by revocation of government grants, annuities, and offices, others by imprisonment or execution on charges that ranged from fraud to treason. It is probable that Chaucer's resignation from his customs position was an attempt to escape being caught in Gloucester's net on some fabricated charge. Several of those who were executed for treason (the charge levied against almost everyone who was particularly close to the King)—

including a young poet, Thomas Usk, and Sir Simon Burley, who had fought beside the Black Prince and had served for years as the King's beloved tutor—were Chaucer's friends. Those were terrible years for Chaucer in other ways, too. Leaving the customs job meant leaving London, where he could not afford to live without his government job, and relocating to Greenwich, in the wild suburbs. His wife, Philippa, died in 1387. With almost no income, he went deeply into debt and was sued several times by his creditors. (385–388) The envoi to "Lack of Steadfastnesse," addressed to the King, suggests, when Richard became king in his own right in 1389, Chaucer undoubtedly looked forward to improved times and conditions for the country.

> O Prince, desire to be honourable,
> Cherice thy folk, and hate extorcion,
> Suffer nothing that may be reprevable
> To thine estate doon in thy region.
> Show forth thy swerd of castigacion,
> Dread God, do law, love, truth, and worthinesse,
> And wed thy folk again to steadfastnesse.

That, however, didn't happen. After a short "honeymoon" period, Richard instituted against those he considered his enemies a reign of retribution that was every bit as harsh as Gloucester's had been. In the process, he alienated almost all his erstwhile supporters. His behavior— one might say his arrogance—would lead first to his deposition, in 1399, and then to his murder, in 1400. Though short, the six-line addition (lines 360–366) that Chaucer made in 1394 to the G version of the prologue to *The Legend of Good Women* speaks volumes about Chaucer's disillusionment with the English court and its king.

THE CANTERBURY TALES

It is certainly no coincidence that Chaucer began writing *The Canterbury Tales* during or immediately following his term in Parliament. It may well be, as Howard argues, that he "began the work as an escape from the outward and inner pressures of his life"; and that within the framework of a pilgrimage "he could think about and laugh at the very fabric of a society that seemed to be falling in pieces." (401) It may also be that, in choosing to write a work that included virtually all known literary genres and took its characters from across the spectrum of English life, he was attempting to make some sense of the dissonance and fragmentation around him by creating the English world as a whole made up of varied parts working together toward a common goal—of getting somewhere. That he was distancing himself from courtly concerns is obvious from much of the *Tales'* subject matter, which would have been inappropriate for or of little interest to a courtly audience. It is strongly suggested also by the fact that in 1389, after accepting the high-paying and prestigious position as a Clerk of the King's Works shortly after Richard attained majority, and when he certainly could have afforded to, he did not move back to London; he maintained his residence in Greenwich. In fact, he did not return to live in London again until December of 1399, *after* Richard's ouster in October of the same year. Whether the Parliament of 1386 was "a turning point in English history" (Howard, 387) is debatable. Certainly, though, it was a turning point for Chaucer, for his life and for his work. It changed his opinion of the English court and broadened his view of the English world. Until now, he had been writing for a courtly audience, but now, living in Greenwich, he envisioned a different audience, in a different world.

There is evidence that some of the *Tales* were being circulated and read by Chaucer's court friends while the work was still in progress— from the state of some of the manuscripts (Howard, 401, 409) and from the short poem "Lenvoy de Chaucer a Bukton," in which the poet refers his friend to the Wife of Bath on the subject of marriage (29–30). Still, the audience that Chaucer had in mind for *The Canterbury Tales* was "a national one" that would have understood "the national cross-section of the General Prologue". (Howard, 407) And the world of that audience was the world of the majority, the middle class of English society, which included neither of the extreme ends of the social spectrum—no royals or upper nobility and no common laborers, excepting the Plowman, who is so idealized as to lose any commonness worthy of the name. That audience clearly was understood to be a male one. Most of the pilgrims are male, and it is to them that the few female travelers speak. The point the Wife of Bath makes about "what women want," for instance, is surely something women didn't need to be told. The maleness of the intended audience of *The Canterbury Tales* is further indicated by its inclusion of such tales as those of the Miller and the Reeve, which are clearly "men's" stories. (Green, "Women," 153) For this new, national audience, Chaucer chose as a frame a nationally recognizable occasion: a pilgrimage to the shrine of a national saint, St. Thomas à Becket, the great saint of the English "people".

The basic outline of the *Canterbury Tales* is simple: on a spring day in April, a group of travelers assemble at the Tabard Inn in Southwark, a suburb of London, to begin a sixty-mile, four-day trip to Canterbury. Over the course of the journey, the travelers tell stories, four each, to "shorten the way." The storytelling is set up as a competition among the pilgrims, with the prize for the best set of stories—those "[t]ales of the best sentence and moost solace", that is, the most moral and the most entertaining—being supper at the expense of the others when they return to the Tabard Inn at the end of their trip. (I, 796–801) Harry Bailly, the capable and amiable proprietor of the Tabard Inn, who acts as their host and guide, holds the series of stories together by calling on the pilgrims for their tales, commenting on both the tales and their tellers, and restoring peace after the travelers' quarrels. They are on a pilgrimage, but they are also on holiday: it's spring, and adventure is in the air. That combination, of a religious occasion and a pleasure trip, brings together a widely disparate group of characters from across the spectrum of middle-class English society—"high and low, old and young, male and female, lay and clerical, learned and ignorant, rogue and righteous, land and sea, town and country" (Coghill, 12)—each of whom is presented in the work's *General Prologue* as both a fourteenth-century "type" and an individual human personality. The gallery of their portraits in the *General Prologue* is generally considered to be the most outstanding series of brief character sketches in all of literature, English or otherwise. Over the course of the trip, both their types and their personalities are further revealed through their interaction with each other and through the tales they tell. Some of their stories are among the finest of their various genres. And the pilgrims' interactions with each other create wonderful drama, for which the *General Prologue* sets the stage but is only the first act. Chaucer declares at the end of *Troilus and Criseyde* that he hopes before he dies to write "some comedy" (V, 1787–88); unfinished and fragmented as *The Canterbury Tales* may be, he certainly met his goal.

STRUCTURE OF THE *TALES*

From the plan set out in its *General Prologue*, which calls for four stories from each of the thirty pilgrims (29 plus the poet), two each way to and from Canterbury, we may assume that Chaucer intended to write a total of 120 tales. Only 24 (and two of these are unfinished) constitute the work as it has survived. Because it is unfinished, and Chaucer left no outline indicating how or where these twenty-four tales "fit" within a work that, based on the *General Prologue*, he intended to be a much larger whole, we have to depend for their sequencing on Chaucer's "literary executors," those early scribes who first assembled the tales in what they felt was their best arrangement. That process was undoubtedly aided to some degree by the fact that some of the tales have prologues within which the pilgrims interact with each other in ways that provide enough clues to indicate that at least some of the tales were intended to be ordered in specific relation to others. These clues, however, go only so far as to allow the tales to be grouped as groups, or "Fragments" (ten of them), not as a whole. Thus, while we can make pretty good guesses about what tales belong to which Fragment and in what order within their Fragment, we have no real clues as to how the Fragments should be arranged in relation to each other. Most modern editions follow the order that Robinson established in his *Complete Works* for the Cambridge Poets series in 1933 (revised in 1957), which in turn follows the arrangement of the tales in the Ellesmere manuscript, a very carefully transcribed (and beautifully illuminated) text that dates to about ten years after Chaucer's death. Beginning with the *General Prologue* and ending with Chaucer's Retraction, this arrangement orders the Fragments as follows: I: Knight, Miller, Reeve, Cook; II: Man of Law; III: Wife of Bath, Friar, Summoner; IV: Clerk, Merchant; V: Squire, Franklin; VI: Physician, Pardoner; VII: Shipman, Prioress, *Sir Thopas*, *Melbee*, Monk, Nun's Priest; VIII: Second Nun, Canon's Yeoman; IX: Manciple; X: Parson. While this order may not be Chaucer's own, it seems to make the most sense of the tales as we have them.

Generically, *The Canterbury Tales* is a collection of short stories. It differs significantly, however, from other story collections known in the fourteenth century, the primary expectations of which were that they would be moral (as were the many known collections of *exempla*, cautionary stories used by preachers) and reasonably homogeneous (as

were the several known collections of particular genres, such as saints'
lives or beast fables); Chaucer's own *Legend of Good Women* is a collection
of exactly this sort. In contrast to the norm for such collections, *The
Canterbury Tales* offers no moral pattern or framework and includes in
the generic and poetic range of its individual tales almost all of the
literary forms that make up the body of work that constitutes Medieval
Literature. Varieties of Romance are illustrated in the tales of the
Knight, the Squire, the Clerk, and the Wife of Bath. Romance is
parodied in *Sir Thopas*. Echoes of the Breton *lai* can be found in the
Franklin's tale. Various forms of the French *fabliau*, a comical and often
obscene story, that is, a socially or politically subversive one, are told by
the Miller, the Reeve, the Shipman, the Summoner, the Cook, and the
Merchant. "The Nun's Priest's Tale" is an exemplary illustration of the
beast fable. The Man of Law and the Physician tell classical legends, and
the Second Nun tells a hagiography or saint's life. The Pardoner and
Friar offer *exempla*; the Prioress recounts a Miracle of the Virgin; and
Chaucer and the Manciple tell moral allegories. The Parson gives a
sermon, and the Canon Yeoman makes a literary confession. Chaucer's
Retraction is an example of the medieval *palinode*, an "I take it back"
statement. The tales divide fairly evenly between the humorous and the
serious. Two are written in prose (*Melibee* and "The Parson's Tale"), the
others in verse. Such variety is unparalleled in any other collection. So,
too, is Chaucer's method of articulating the stories: via the pilgrimage
and the competition. The framework of a pilgrimage allows him to
assemble a variety of people to match the variety of their tales, and the
competition, by insisting on the importance of both aesthetic and
didactic excellence, allows him to present, not very subtly, the case for
his being the writer of the "best of" most of the genres known in his
time.

    In contrast also to the prologues of most other collections, the
General Prologue of *The Canterbury Tales* does not directly introduce the
kinds of stories to be told; rather, it introduces the people who will tell
them, people who are themselves defined by the variety that makes up
the social spectrum they represent. Though the Host seems at first to
have the idea that he can impose some sort of order on these people by
selecting the Monk to follow the Knight, so that the tale-telling might
"proceed properly" (I, 3131), his plans are quickly foiled by the Miller's
interruption, which establishes an interactive rather than a hierarchical
ordering of the tales. This is not the world of the court, dominated by

rank. It is the larger and largely unstable world of a rapidly changing post-Plague England: where Wycliff and his followers were questioning the institutional beliefs and moral character of the Church; where long-standing feudal institutions were crumbling under the pressure of peasants demanding the most basic rights; and where the emergence of a middle class meant that money was replacing land and rank as the grease to the social machine. These are impatient and often unruly pilgrims, unwilling to stand humbly by and wait for their designated turns. That the Knight's tale (a romance) is followed by the Miller's (a *fabliau*), in disregard of both social hierarchy and poetic consistency, announces the key to the work's overall theme and method: that it will offer contrasting views of the human experience. The Knight and Miller present the extremes of that experience. Though their tales share an almost identical plot, they operate in very different worlds: one raises questions about the providential ordering of the universe, and the other refuses to look beyond the individual's immediate interest. Different genres offer different readings of the world and of the subject's experience of it. (Cooper, 17–19, 101–103)

THEMES AND TONE OF THE *TALES*

Most of the themes, motifs, and ideas contained in the *Tales* are first presented, albeit from differing perspectives and to differing degrees, by its first two tellers: questions disallowed by the official faith as to the nature of the providential ordering of the world; the suffering of innocents; what human beings most desire; the nature of love; what constitutes friendship; what makes a good ruler; what defines a good life; and the role of women in marriage. The motif of ecclesiastical corruption is introduced later, in the Friar's Tale. As the tales accumulate, these themes and motifs interplay and coexist with each other in ways that both celebrate and reject convention and orthodoxy. In some cases a tale may follow directly from its predecessor and cue its sequel or its opposite, as the Miller's connects the Knight's and the Reeve's; as the Summoner's tale continues his quarrel with the Friar; and as the Merchant's May responds to the Clerk's Griselde. In other cases, similar themes, ideas, and motifs are taken up by tales at some distance from each other, as when the Clerk responds to the Wife of Bath two tales later; and when, still later, the Franklin responds to them both.

Each genre defines its own vocabulary and imagery, its own area of experience, and its own way of signifying that experience, which sets up a secondary theme that runs throughout the *Tales*: the difficulty of establishing either the "truth" or the "reality" of an experience when the verbal means of expressing them are so unreliable: different genres give different readings of the world. This is demonstrated by the differing ways that the pilgrims interpret their companions' stories, and it is addressed quite directly in the Manciple's Tale's discussion of how word choices influence moral reactions. (Cooper, 19)

Some of the tales, such as the Miller's and the Shipman's, are highly entertaining; others, such as the Monk's and the Clerk's, are not, even by medieval standards. The Prioress' Tale, with its appalling but unfortunately conventional medieval anti-Semitism, makes us very uncomfortable. The Wife of Bath's tales—as she really tells two stories, both the engaging account of her five marriages (in her prologue) and her tale of a rapist knight who is rewarded with a happy marriage to a beautiful young woman—are at once entertaining and alarming. "The Nun's Priest's Tale" is on the whole a wonderfully charming example of a beast fable; its humorous reference to one of the most horrific events of Chaucer's lifetime—the brutal massacre of 35 innocent Flemish workers during the Peasants' Revolt in 1381—as part of an almost offhand four-line description of the noise of the local villagers as they pursued the fox (III, 3394–97), however, demonstrates a clear disregard for human life.

"A Purveyor of God's Plenty"

Lee Patterson distinguishes between two Chaucers: "one is a fourteenth-century writer whose every word requires elaborate annotation, while the other is a purveyor of God's plenty ... who speaks with an immediacy that obviates the need for interpretation." (18) This is a gross understatement. There are many Chaucers: the sophisticated and learned Chaucer; the ironic Chaucer; the feminist Chaucer; the anti-feminist Chaucer; the rhetorical Chaucer; the social Chaucer; the gloomy Chaucer; the pious Chaucer; the literary Chaucer. And there is the Chaucer who is not serious enough because he enjoys telling stories about "hot coulters, bare bottoms and swyved wives." (Garbáty, 173) Chaucer would certainly appreciate so very many constructions of the "real" or "true" Chaucer, and would probably agree with all of the above, excepting the last. If there is one thing that Chaucer *is*, it's serious—about his poetry, whatever its content. Indeed, as poets go, he is inordinately fond of reminding us not only of what he has written—as he does in the catalogues of his work-to-date in the Prologues to *The Legend of Good Women* and "The Man of Law's Tale" in *The Canterbury Tales*—but also of how very good a writer he is—as he does with the framework of a storytelling competition in the *Tales*. Even in his very carefully written-in-advance deathbed retraction at the end of the *Tales* of those works that "sounen [tend] into sin," he takes great pains to name every one of those he doesn't want "saved," lest any be overlooked and left out of his official canon. We can't know whether the *poet* has been "saved," but we can be grateful that his work has.

NOTE

1.   Unless otherwise noted, quotations from Chaucer's works come from The Riverside Chaucer, Larry D. Benson, ed.

WORKS CITED

Baugh, Albert. *Chaucer's Major Poetry*. New York: Appleton-Century-Crofts, 1963.

————, and Thomas Cable. *A History of the English Language*. 4th ed. Englewood Cliffs, New Jersey: Prentice Hall, 1993.

Benson, Larry D., ed. *The Riverside Chaucer*. Boston: Houghton Mifflin, 1987.

Brewer, Derek. *A New Introduction to Chaucer*. 2d ed. New York: Addison Wesley Longman, 1998.

Coghill, Neville. *Chaucer: The Canterbury Tales*. Baltimore: Penguin, 1952.

Cooper, Helen. *Oxford Guides To Chaucer: The Canterbury Tales*. New York: Oxford University Press, 1989.

Donaldson, E. Talbot. "Chaucer and the Elusion of Clarity." *Essays and Studies 1972 in Honour of Beatrice White*. Ed. T.S. Dorsch. New York: Humanities Press, 1972. 23–44.

———. *Chaucer's Poetry: An Anthology for the Modern Reader*. 2d ed. New York: Ronald Press, 1975.

Fisher, John. "A Language Policy for Lancastrian England." *Writing After Chaucer*. Ed. Daniel J. Pinti. New York: Garland, 1998. 81–99.

Garbáty, Thomas J. "Chaucer and Comedy." *Versions of Medieval Comedy*. Ed. Paul Ruggiers. Norman: University of Oklahoma Press, 1977. 173–190.

Green, Richard Firth. *Poets and Prince Pleasers: Literature and the English Court in the Late Middle Ages*. Toronto: University of Toronto Press, 1980.

———. "Women in Chaucer's Audience." *Chaucer Review* 18 (1983): 146–154.

Hoccleve, Thomas. "The Regement of Princes." *Hoccleve's Works*. Vol. 3. Ed. F.J. Furnivall. Oxford: Early English Text Society, 1897.

Howard, Donald. *Chaucer: His Life, His Works, His World*. New York: Fawcett Columbine, 1987.

Kittredge, George Lyman. *Chaucer and His Poetry*. London: Oxford University Press, 1915.

Patterson, Lee. *Negotiating the Past: The Historical Understanding of Medieval Literature*. Madison: University of Wisconsin Press, 1987.

Shoaf, R.A. *Geoffrey Chaucer: Troilus and Criseyde*. East Lansing, Michigan: Colleagues Press, 1989.

Strohm, Paul. *Social Chaucer*. Cambridge: Harvard University Press, 1994.

Tuchman, Barbara. *A Distant Mirror: The Calamitous Fourteenth Century*. New York: Knopf, 1978.

GEORGE LYMAN KITTREDGE

Chaucer's Discussion of Marriage

We are prone to read and study the *Canterbury Tales* as if each tale were an isolated unit and to pay scant attention to what we call the connecting links,—those bits of lively narrative and dialogue that bind the whole together. Yet Chaucer's plan is clear enough. Structurally regarded, the *Canterbury Tales* is a kind of Human Comedy. From this point of view, the Pilgrims are the *dramatis personae*, and their stories are only speeches that are somewhat longer than common, entertaining in and for themselves (to be sure), but primarily significant, in each case, because they illustrate the speaker's character and opinions, or show the relations of the travelers to one another in the progressive action of the Pilgrimage. In other words, we ought not merely to consider the general appropriateness of each tale to the character of the teller: we should also inquire whether the tale is not determined to some extent, by the circumstances,—by the situation at the moment, by something that another Pilgrim has said or done, by the turn of a discussion already under way.

Now and then, to be sure, the point is too obvious to be overlooked, as in the squabble between the Summoner and the Friar and that between the Reeve and the Miller, in the Shipman's intervening to check the Parson, and in the way in which the gentles head off the Pardoner when he is about to tell a ribald anecdote. But despite these inescapable

Kittredge, George Lyman, "Chaucer's Discussion of Marriage." *Modern Philology*, IX (1911 1912), 135–67 (University of Chicago Press).

instances, the general principle is too often blinked or ignored. Yet its temperate application should clear up a number of things which are traditionally regarded as difficulties, or as examples of heedlessness on Chaucer's part.

Without attempting to deny or abridge the right to study and criticize each tale in and for itself,—as legend, romance, *exemplum*, fabliau, or what-not,—and without extenuating the results that this method has achieved, let us consider certain tales in their relation to Chaucer's structural plan,—with reference, that is to say, to the Pilgrims who tell them and to the Pilgrimage to which their telling is accidental. We may begin with the story of Griselda.

This is a plain and straightforward piece of edification, and nobody has ever questioned its appropriateness to the Clerk, who, as he says himself, has traveled in Italy and has heard it from the lips of the laureate Petrarch. The Clerk's 'speech,' according to the General Prologue, was 'sowning in moral vertu,' so that this story is precisely the kind of thing which we should expect from his lips. True, we moderns sometimes feel shocked or offended at what we style the immorality of Griselda's unvarying submission. But this feeling is no ground of objection to the appropriateness of the tale to the Clerk. The Middle Ages delighted (as children still delight) in stories, that exemplify a single human quality, like valor, or tyranny, or fortitude. In such cases, the settled rule (for which neither Chaucer nor the Clerk was responsible) was to show to what lengths that quality may conceivably go. Hence, in tales of this kind, there can be no question of conflict between duties, no problem as to the point at which excess of goodness becomes evil. It is, then, absurd to censure a fourteenth-century Clerk for telling (or Chaucer for making him tell) a story which exemplifies in this hyperbolical way the virtue of fortitude under affliction. Whether Griselda could have put an end to her woes, or ought to have put an end to them, by refusing to obey her husband's commands is *parum ad rem*. We are to look at her trials as inevitable, and to pity her accordingly, and wonder at her endurance. If we refuse to accept the tale in this spirit, we are ourselves the losers. We miss the pathos because we are aridly intent on discussing an ethical question that has no status in this particular court, however pertinent it may be in the general forum of morals.

Furthermore, in thus focusing attention on the morality or immorality of Griselda's submissiveness, we overlook what the Clerk takes pains to make as clear as possible,—the real lesson that the story is meant to convey,—and thus we do grave injustice to that austere but amiable moralist. The Clerk, a student of 'Aristotle and his philosophye,' knew as well as any of us that every virtue may be conceived as a mean between two extremes. Even the Canon's Yeoman, an ignorant man, was aware of this principle:

> 'That that is overdoon, it wol nat preve
> Aright, as clerkes seyn,—it is a vyce.'

Chaucer had too firm a grasp on his *dramatis personae* to allow the Clerk to leave the true purpose of his parable undefined. 'This story is not told,' says the Clerk in substance, 'to exhort wives to imitate Griselda's humility, for *that* would be beyond the capacity of human nature. It is told in order that every man or woman, in whatever condition of life, may learn fortitude in adversity. For, since a woman once exhibited such endurance under trials inflicted on her by a mortal man, *a fortiori* ought *we* to accept patiently whatever tribulation God may send us. For God is not like Griselda's husband. He does not wantonly experiment with us, out of inhuman scientific curiosity. God *tests* us, as it is reasonable that our Maker should test his handiwork, but he does not *tempt* us. He allows us to be beaten with sharp scourges of adversity, not, like the Marquis Walter, to see if we can stand it, for he knoweth our frame, he remembereth that we are dust: all his affliction is for our better grace. Let us live, therefore, in manly endurance of the visitations of Providence.'

And then, at verse 1163, comes that matchless passage in which the Clerk (having explained the *universal* application of his parable,—having provided with scrupulous care against any misinterpretation of its serious purport) turns with gravely satiric courtesy to the Wife of Bath and makes the particular application of the story to her 'life' and 'all her sect.'

Here one may appreciate the vital importance of considering the *Canterbury Tales* as a connected Human Comedy,—of taking into account the Pilgrims in their relations to one another in the great drama to which the several narratives are structurally incidental. For it is precisely at this point that Professor Skeat notes a difficulty. 'From this point to the end,' he remarks, 'is the work of a later period, and in Chaucer's best manner, though unsuited *to the coy Clerk*.' This is as much as to say that, in the remaining stanzas of the Clerk's Tale and in the

Envoy, Chaucer has violated dramatic propriety. And, indeed, many readers have detected in these concluding portions Chaucer's own personal revulsion of feeling against the tale that he had suffered the Clerk to tell.

Now the supposed difficulty vanishes as soon as we study vvs. 1163–1212, not as an isolate phenomenon, but in their relation to the great drama of the Canterbury Pilgrimage. It disappears when we consider the lines in what we may call their dramatic context, that is (to be specific), when we inquire what there was in the situation to prompt the Clerk, after emphasizing the serious and universal moral of Griselda's story, to give his tale a special and peculiar application by annexing an ironical tribute to the Wife of Bath, her life, her 'sect,' and her principles. To answer this question we must go back to the Wife of Bath's Prologue.

The Wife of Bath's Prologue begins a Group in the *Canterbury Tales*, or, as one may say, a new act in the drama. It is not connected with anything that precedes. Let us trace the action from this point down to the moment when the Clerk turns upon the Wife with his satirical compliments.

The Wife has expounded her views at great length and with all imaginable zest. Virginity, which the Church glorifies, is not required of us. Our bodies are given us to use. Let saints be continent if they will. She has no wish to emulate them. Nor does she accept the doctrine that a widow or a widower must not marry again. Where is bigamy forbidden in the Bible, or octogamy either? She has warmed both hands before the fire of life, and she exults in her recollection of her fleshly delights.

True, she is willing to admit, for convention's sake, that chastity is the ideal state. But it is not *her* ideal. On the contrary, her admission is only for appearances. In her heart she despises virginity. Her contempt for it is thinly veiled, or rather, not veiled at all. Her discourse is marked by frank and almost obstreperous animalism. Her whole attitude is that of scornful, though good-humored, repudiation of what the Church teaches in that regard.

Nor is the Wife content with this single heresy. She maintains also that wives should rule their husbands, and she enforces this doctrine by an account of her own life, and further illustrates it by her tale of the knight of King Arthur who learned that

Wommen desiren to have sovereyntee
As wel over hir housbond as hir love,
And for to been in maistrie him above,

and who accepted the lesson as sound doctrine. Then, at the end of her discourse, she sums up in no uncertain words:

And Iesu Crist us sende
Housbandes meke, yonge, and fresshe abedde,
And grace to overbyde hem that we wedde;
And eek I preye Iesu shorte her lyves
That wol nat be governed by her wyves.

Now the Wife of Bath is not *bombinans in vacuo*. She addresses her heresies not to *us* or to the world at large, but to her fellow-pilgrims. Chaucer has made this point perfectly clear. The words of the Wife were of a kind to provoke comment,—and we have the comment. The Pardoner interrupts her with praise of her noble preaching:

'Now, dame,' quod he, 'by God and by seint Iohn,
Ye been a noble prechour in this cas!'

The adjective is not accidental. The Pardoner was a judge of good preaching: the General Prologue describes him as 'a noble ecclesiaste' and he shows his ability in his own sermon on Covetousness. Furthermore, it is the Friar's comment on the Wife's preamble that provokes the offensive words of the Summoner, and that becomes thereby the occasion for the two tales that immediately follow in the series. It is manifest, then, that Chaucer meant us to imagine the *dramatis personae* as taking a lively interest in whatever the Wife says. This being so, we ought to inquire what effect her Prologue and Tale would have upon the Clerk.

Of course the Clerk was scandalized. He was unworldly and an ascetic,—he 'looked holwe and therto sobrely.' Moral virtue was his special study. He had embraced the celibate life. He was grave, devout, and unflinchingly orthodox. And now he was confronted by the lust of the flesh and the pride of life in the person of a woman who flouted chastity and exulted that she had 'had her world as in her time.' Nor was this all. The woman was an heresiarch, or at best a schismatic. She set up, and aimed to establish, a new and dangerous sect, whose principle was that the wife should rule the husband. The Clerk kept silence for the moment. Indeed, he had no chance to utter his sentiments, unless he interrupted,—something not to be expected of his quiet ('coy') and sober temperament. But it is not to be imagined that his thoughts were idle. He could be trusted to speak to the purpose whenever his opportunity should come.

Now the substance of the Wife's false doctrines was not the only thing that must have roused the Clerk to protesting answer. The very manner of her discourse was a direct challenge to him. She had garnished her sermon with scraps of Holy Writ and rags and tatters of erudition, caught up, we may infer, from her last husband. Thus she had put herself into open competition with the guild of scholars and theologians, to which the Clerk belonged. Further, with her eye manifestly upon this sedate philosopher, she had taken pains to gird at him and his fellows. At first she pretends to be modest and apologetic,— 'so that the clerkes be nat with me wrothe,'—but later she abandons all pretense and makes an open attack:

> 'For trusteth wel, it is an impossible
> That any clerk wol speken good of wyves,
> But—if it be of holy seintes lyves,
> Ne of noon other womman never the mo....
>
> The clerk, whan he is old, and may noght do
> Of Venus werkes worth his olde sho,
> Than sit he doun, and writ in his dotage
> That wommen can nat kepe his mariage.'

And there was more still that the Wife made our Clerk endure. Her fifth husband was, like him, a 'clerk of Oxenford'—surely this is no accidental coincidence on Chaucer's part. He had abandoned his studies ('had left scole'), and had given up all thought of taking priest's orders. The Wife narrates, with uncommon zest, how she intrigued with him, and cajoled him, and married him (though he was twenty and she was forty), and how finally she made him utterly subservient to her will,—how she got 'by maistrye al the soveraynetee.' This was gall and wormwood to our Clerk. The Wife not only trampled on his principles in her theory and practice, but she pointed her attack by describing how she had subdued to her heretical sect a clerk of Oxenford, an alumnus of our Clerk's own university. The Wife's discourse is not malicious. She is too jovial to be ill-natured, and she protests that she speaks in jest. But it none the less embodies a rude personal assault upon the Clerk, whose quiet mien and habitual reticence made him seem a safe person to attack. She had done her best to make the Clerk ridiculous. He saw it; the company saw it. He kept silent, biding his time.

All this is not speculation. It is nothing but straightforward interpretation of the text in the light of the circumstances and the situation. We can reject it only by insisting on the manifest absurdity (shown to be such in every headlink and endlink) that Chaucer did not visualize the Pilgrims whom he had been at such pains to describe in the Prologue, and that he never regarded them as associating, as looking at each other and thinking of each other, as becoming better and better acquainted as they jogged along the Canterbury road.

Chaucer might have given the Clerk a chance to reply to the Wife immediately. But he was too good an artist. The drama of the Pilgrimage is too natural and unforced in its development under the master's hand to admit of anything so frigidly schematic. The very liveliness with which he conceived his individual *dramatis personae* forbade. The Pilgrims were interested in the Wife's harangue, but it was for the talkative members of the company to thrust themselves forward. The Pardoner had already interrupted her with humorous comments before she was fully under way and had exhorted her to continue her account of the 'praktike' of marriage. The Friar, we may be confident, was on good terms with her before she began; she was one of those 'worthy wommen of the toun' whom he especially cultivated. He, too, could not refrain from comment:

> The Frere lough, whan he had herd al this:
> 'Now, dame,' quod he, 'so have I ioye or blis,
> This is a long preamble of a tale!'

The Summoner reproved him, in words that show not only his professional enmity but also the amusement that the Pilgrims in general were deriving from the Wife's disclosures. They quarreled, and each threatened to tell a story at the other's expense. Then the Host intervened roughly, calling for silence and bidding the Wife go ahead with her story. She assented, but not without a word of good-humored, though ironical, deference to the Friar:

> 'Al redy, sir,' quod she, 'right as yow lest,
> If I have license of this worthy Frere.'

And, at the very beginning of her tale, she took humorous vengeance for his interruption in a characteristic bit of satire at the expense of 'limitours and other holy freres.' This passage, we note, has nothing whatever to do with her tale. It is a side-remark in which she is talking at the Friar, precisely as she has talked at the Clerk in her prologue.

The quarrel between the Summoner and the Friar was in abeyance until the Wife finished her tale. They let her end her story and proclaim her moral in peace,—the same heretical doctrine that we have already noted, that the wife should be the head of the house. Then the Friar spoke, and his words are very much to our present purpose. He adverts in significant terms both to the subject and to the manner of the Wife's discourse,—a discourse, we should observe, that was in effect a doctrinal sermon illustrated (as the fashion of preachers was) by a pertinent *exemplum*:

> 'Ye have here touched, al-so moot I thee,
> In scole-matere great difficultee.'

She has handled a hard subject that properly belongs to scholars. She has quoted authorities, too, like a clerk. Such things, he says, are best left to ecclesiastics:

> 'But, dame, here as we ryden by the weye,
> Us nedeth nat to speken but of game,
> And lete auctoritees, on Goddes name,
> To preching and to scole eek of clergye.'

This, to be sure, is but a device to 'conveyen his matere,'—to lead up to his proposal to 'telle a game' about a summoner. But it serves to recall our minds to the Wife's usurpation of clerkly functions. If we think of the Clerk at all at this point (and assuredly Chaucer had not forgotten him), we must feel that here is another prompting (undesigned though it be on the Friar's part) to take up the subject which the Wife has (in the Clerk's eyes) so shockingly maltreated.

Then follows the comic interlude of the Friar and the Summoner, in the course of which we may perhaps lose sight of the serious subject which the Wife had set abroach,—the status of husband and wife in the marriage relation. But Chaucer did not lose sight of it. It was a part of his design that the Host should call on the Clerk for the first story of the next day.

This is the opportunity for which the Clerk has been waiting. He has not said a word in reply to the Wife's heresies or to her personal attack on him and his order. Seemingly she has triumphed. The subject has apparently been dismissed with the Friar's words about leaving such matters to sermons and to school debates. The Host, indeed, has no idea that the Clerk proposes to revive the discussion; he does not even think of the Wife in calling upon the representative of that order which has fared so ill at her hands.

> 'Sir clerk of Oxenford,' our hoste sayde,
> 'Ye ryde as coy and stille as doth a mayde
> Were newe spoused, sitting at the bord;
> This day ne herd I of your tonge a word.
> I trowe ye studie about som sophyme.'

Even here there is a suggestion (casual, to be sure, and, so far as the Host is concerned, quite unintentional) of *marriage*, the subject which is occupying the Clerk's mind. For the Host is mistaken. The Clerk's abstraction is only apparent. He is not pondering syllogisms; he is biding his time.

'Tell us a tale,' the unconscious Host goes on, 'but don't preach us a Lenten sermon—tell us som mery thing of aventures.' 'Gladly,' replies the demure scholar. 'I will tell you a story that a worthy *clerk* once told me at Padua—Francis Petrarch, God rest his soul!'

At this word *clerk*, pronounced with grave and inscrutable emphasis, the Wife of Bath must have pricked up her ears. But she has no inkling of what is in store, nor is the Clerk in any hurry to enlighten her. He opens with tantalizing deliberation, and it is not until he has spoken more than sixty lines that he mentions marriage. 'The Marquis Walter,' says the Clerk, 'lived only for the present and lived for pleasure only'—

'As for to hauke and hunte on every syde,
Wel ny al othere cures leet he slyde;
And eek he nolde, and that was worst of alle,
Wedde no wyf, for noght that may bifalle.'

These words may or may not have appeared significant to the company at large. To the Wife of Bath, at all events, they must have sounded interesting. And when, in a few moments, the Clerk made Walter's subjects speak of 'soveraynetee,' the least alert of the Pilgrims can hardly have missed the point:

'Boweth your nekke under that blisful yok
Of soveraynetee, noght of servyse,
Which that men clepeth spousialle or wedlock.'

'Sovereignty' had been the Wife's own word:

'And whan that I hadde geten unto me
By maistrie al the soveraynetee';

'Wommen desyren to have soveryntee
As wel over his housband as hir love,
And for to been in maistrie him above.'

Clearly the Clerk is catching up the subject proposed by the Wife. The discussion is under way again.

Yet despite the cheerful view that Walter's subjects take of the marriage yoke, it is by no means yet clear to the Wife of Bath and the other Pilgrims what the Clerk is driving at. For he soon makes Walter declare that 'liberty is seldom found in marriage,' and that if he weds a wife, he must exchange freedom for servitude. Indeed, it is not until vvs. 351–57 are reached that Walter reveals himself as a man who is determined to rule his wife absolutely. From that point to the end there is no room for doubt in any Pilgrim's mind: *the Clerk is answering the Wife of Bath*; he is telling of a woman whose principles in marriage were the antithesis of hers; he is reasserting the orthodox view in opposition to the heresy which she had expounded with such zest and with so many flings and jeers at the clerkly profession and character.

What is the tale of Griselda? Several things, no doubt—an old *märchen*, an *exemplum*, a *novella*, what you will. Our present concern, however, is primarily with the question what it seemed to be to the Canterbury Pilgrims, told as it was by an individual Clerk of Oxford at a particular moment and under the special circumstances. The answer is plain. To them it was a retort (indirect, impersonal, masterly) to the Wife of Bath's heretical doctrine that the woman should be the head of the man. It told them of a wife who had no such views,—who promised ungrudging obedience and kept her vow. The Wife of Bath had railed at her husbands and badgered them and cajoled them: Griselda never lost her patience or her serenity. On its face, then, the tale appeared to the Pilgrims to be a dignified and scholarly narrative, derived from a great Italian clerk who was dead, and now utilized by their fellow-pilgrim, the Clerk of Oxford, to demolish the heretical structure so boisterously reared by the Wife of Bath in her prologue and her tale.

But Chaucer's Clerk was a logician—'unto logik hadde he longe ygo.' He knew perfectly well that the real moral of his story was not that which his hearers would gather. He was aware that Griselda was no model for literal imitation by ordinary womankind. If so taken, his tale proved too much; it reduced his argument *ad absurdum*. If he let it go at that, he was playing into his opponent's hands. Besides, he was a conscientious man. He could not misrepresent the lesson which Petrarch had meant to teach and had so clearly expressed,—the lesson of submissive fortitude under tribulation sent by God. Hence he does not fail to explain this moral fully and in unmistakable terms, and to refer distinctly to Petrarch as authority for it:

And herkeneth what this auctor seith therefore.

This is seyd, nat for that wyves sholde
Folwen Griselde as in humilitee,
For it were importable, though they wolde;
But that for every wight, in his degree,
Sholde be constant in adversitee
As was Grisilde; therfor Petrark wryteth
This storie, which with heigh style he endyteth.

For, sith a womman was so pacient
Un-to a mortal man, wel more us ogthe

> Receyven al in gree that God us sent;
> For greet skile is, he preve that he wroghte.
> But he no tempteth no man that he boghte,
> As seith sent Iame, if ye his pistel rede;
> He preveth folk al day, it is no drede,
>
> And suffreth us, as for our exercyse,
> With sharpe scourges of adversitee
> Ful often to be bete in sondry wyse;
> Nat for to knowe our wil, for certes he,
> Er we were born, knew at our freletee;
> And for our beste is at his governaunce:
> Lat us than live in vertuous suffrance.

Yet the Clerk has no idea of failing to make his point against the Wife of Bath. And so, when the tale is finished and the proper Petrarchan moral has been duly elaborated, he turns to the Wife (whom he has thus far sedulously refrained from addressing) and distinctly applies the material to the purpose of an ironical answer, of crushing force, to her whole heresy. There is nothing inappropriate to his character in this procedure. Quite the contrary. Clerks were always satirizing women—the Wife had said so herself—and this particular Clerk had, of course, no scruples against using the powerful weapon of irony in the service of religion and 'moral vertu.' In this instance, the satire is peculiarly poignant for two reasons: first, because it comes with all the suddenness of a complete change of tone (from high seriousness to biting irony, and from the impersonal to the personal); and secondly, because in the tale which he has told, the Clerk had incidentally refuted a false statement of the Wife's, to the effect that

> 'It is an impossible
> That any clerk wol speke good of wyves,
> But if it be of holy seintes Iyves,
> No of noon other womman never the mo.'

Clerks *can* 'speak well' of women (as our Clerk has shown), and when women deserve it; and he now proceeds to show that they can likewise speak well (with biting irony) of women who do not deserve it—such women as the Wife of Bath and all her sect of domestic revolutionists.

It now appears that the form and spirit of the conclusion and the Envoy are not only appropriate to clerks in general, but peculiarly and exquisitely appropriate to this particular clerk under these particular circumstances and with this particular task in hand,—the duty of defending the orthodox view of the relations between husband and wife against the heretical opinions of the Wife of Bath: 'One word in conclusion, gentlemen. There are few Griseldas now-a-days. Most women will break before they will bend. Our companion, the Wife of Bath, is an example, as she has told us herself. Therefore, though I cannot sing, I will recite a song in honor, not of Griselda (as you might perhaps expect), but of the Wife of Bath, of the sect of which she aspires to be a doctor, and of the life which she exemplifies in practice—

'For the wyves love of Bathe,
Whos lif and al hir secte God mayntene
In high maistrye, and elles were it scathe.'

Her *way of life*—she had set it forth with incomparable zest. Her *sect*— she was an heresiarch or at least a schismatic. The terms are not accidental: they are chosen with all the discrimination that befits a scholar and a rhetorician. They refer us back (as definitely as the words 'Wife of Bath' themselves) to that prologue in which the Wife had stood forth as an opponent of the orthodox view of subordination in marriage, as the upholder of an heretical doctrine, and as the exultant practicer of what she preached.

And then comes the Clerk's Envoy, the song that he recites in honor of the Wife and all her sect, with its polished lines, its ingenious rhyming, and its utter felicity of scholarly diction. Nothing could be more in character. To whom in all the world could such a masterpiece of rhetoric be appropriate if not to the Clerk of Oxenford? It is a mock encomium, a sustained ironical commendation of what the Wife has taught.

'O noble wives, let no clerk ever have occasion to write such a story of you as Petrarch once told me about Griselda. Follow your great leader, the Wife of Bath. Rule your husbands, as she did; rail at them, as she did; make them jealous, as she did; exert yourselves to get lovers, as she did. And all this you must do whether you are fair or foul [with manifest allusion to the problem of beauty of ugliness presented in the Wife's story]. Do this, I say, and you will fulfil the precepts that she has set forth and achieve the great end which she has proclaimed as the object of marriage: that is, *you will make your husbands miserable, as she did*!'

'Be ay of chere as fight as leef on linde,
And let him care and wepe and wringe and waille!'

And the Merchant (hitherto silent, but not from inattention) catches up the closing words in a gust of bitter passion:

'Weping and wayling, care and other sorwe
I know ynough on even and amorwe.'
Quod the Merchant, 'and so don othere mo
That wedded ben.'

The Clerk's Envoy, then, is not only appropriate to his character and to the situation: it has also a marked dynamic value. For it is this ironical tribute to the Wife of Bath and her dogmas that, with complete dramatic inevitability, calls out the Merchant's *cri de coeur*. The Merchant has no thought of telling a tale at this moment. He is a stately and imposing person in his degree, by no means prone (so the Prologue informs us) to expose any holes there may be in his coat. But he is suffering a kind of emotional crisis. The poignant irony of the Clerk, following hard upon the moving story of a patient and devoted wife, is too much for him. He has just passed through his honeymoon (but two months wed!) and he has sought a respite from his thraldom under color of a pilgrimage to St. Thomas.

'I have a wyf, the worste that may be!'

She would be an overmatch for the devil himself. He need not specify her evil traits: she is bad in every respect.

'There is a long and large difference
Bitwix Grisildis grete pacience
And of my wyf the passing crueltee.'

The Host, as ever, is on the alert. He scents a good story:

'Sin ye so muchel knowen of that art,
Ful hertely I pray yow telle us part.'

The Merchant agrees, as in duty bound, for all the Pilgrims take care
never to oppose the Host, lest he exact the heavy forfeit established as
the penalty for rebellion. But he declines to relate his own experiences,
thus leaving us to infer, if we choose,—for nowhere is Chaucer's artistic
reticence more effective,—that his bride has proved false to him, like the
wife of the worthy Knight of Lombardy.

And so the discussion of marriage is once more in full swing. The
Wife of Bath, without intending it, has opened a debate in which the
Pilgrims have become so absorbed that they will not leave it till the
subject is 'bolted to the bran.'

The Merchant's Tale presents very noteworthy features, and has
been much canvassed, though never (it seems) with due attention to its
plain significance in the Human Comedy of the *Canterbury Tales*. In
substance, it is nothing but a tale of bawdry, one of the most familiar of
its class. There is nothing novel about it except its setting, but that is
sufficiently remarkable. Compare the tale with any other version of the
Pear-Tree Story,—their name is legion,—and its true significance comes
out in striking fashion. The simple fabliau devised by its first author
merely to make those laugh whose lungs are tickle o' the sere, is so
expanded and overlaid with savage satire that it becomes a complete
disquisition of marriage from the only point of view which is possible for
the disenchanted Merchant. Thus considered, the cynicism of the
Merchant's Tale is seen to be in no way surprising, and (to answer
another kind of comment which this piece has evoked) in no sense
expressive of Chaucer's own sentiments, or even of Chaucer's
momentary mood. The cynicism is the Merchant's. It is no more
Chaucer's than Iago's cynicism about love is Shakespeare's.

In a word, the tale is the perfect expression of the Merchant's
angry disgust at his own evil fate and at his folly in bringing that fate
upon himself. Thus, its very lack of restraint—the savagery of the whole,
which has revolted so many readers—is dramatically inevitable. The
Merchant has schooled himself to his debts and his troubles. He is
professionally adept at putting a good face on matters, as every clever
business man must be. But when once the barrier is broken, reticence is
at an end. His disappointment is too fresh, his disillusion has been too
abrupt, for him to measure his words. He speaks in a frenzy of contempt

and hatred. The hatred is for women; the contempt is for himself and all other fools who will not take warning by example. For we should not forget that the satire is aimed at January rather than at May. That egotistical old dotard is less excusable than his young wife, and meets with less mercy at the Merchant's hands.

That the Merchant begins with an encomium on marriage which is one of the most amazing instances of sustained irony in all literature, is not to be wondered at. In the first place, he is ironical because the Clerk has been ironical. Here the connection is remarkably close. The Merchant has fairly snatched the words out of the Clerk's mouth ('And lat him care and wepe and wringe and waille'—'Weping and wayling, care and other sorwe'), and his mock encomium on the wedded state is a sequel to the Clerk's mock encomium on the Wife of Bath's life and all her sect. The spirit is different, but that is quite proper. For the Clerk's satire is the irony of a logician and a moral philosopher, the irony of the intellect and the ethical sense: the Merchant's is the irony of a mere man, it is the irony of passion and personal experience. The Clerk is a theorist,—he looks at the subject from a point of philosophical detachment. The Merchant is an egotist,—he feels himself to be the dupe whose folly he depicts. We may infer, if we like, that he was a man in middle age and that he had married a young wife.

There is plenty of evidence that the Merchant has been an attentive listener. One detects, for instance, a certain similarity between January and the Marquis Walter (different as they are) in that they have both shown themselves disinclined to marriage. Then again, the assertion that a wife is never weary of attending a sick husband—

'She nis nat wery him to love and serve,
Thogh that he lye bedrede til be sterve'—

must have reminded the Pilgrims of poor Thomas, in the Summoner's Tale, whose wife's complaints to her spiritual visitor had precipitated so tremendous a sermon. But such things are trifles compared with the attention which the Merchant devotes to the Wife of Bath.

So far, in this act of Chaucer's Human Comedy, we have found that the Wife of Bath is, in a very real sense, the dominant figure. She has dictated the theme and inspired or instigated the actors; and she has always been at or near the center of the stage. It was a quarrel over her prologue that elicited the tale of the Friar and that of the Summoner. It was she who caused the Clerk to tell of Griselda—and the Clerk satirizes her in his Envoy. 'The art' of which the Host begs the Merchant to tell is *her* art, the art of marriage on which she has discoursed so learnedly. That the Merchant, therefore, should allude to her, quote her words, and finally mention her in plain terms is precisely what was to be expected.

The order and method of these approaches on the Merchant's part are exquisitely natural and dramatic. First there are touches, more or less palpable, when he describes the harmony of wedded life in terms so different from the Wife's account of what her husbands had to endure. Then—after a little—comes a plain enough allusion (put into January's mouth) to the Wife's character, to her frequent marriages, and to her inclination to marry again, old as she is:

> 'And eek thise olde widwes, God it wot,
> They conne so muchel craft on Wades boot,
> So muchel broken harm, whan that hem leste,
> That with hem sholde I never live in reste!
> For sondry scoles maken sotil clerkis:
> Wommen of many scoles half a clerk is.'

Surely the Wife of Bath was a woman of many schools, and her emulation of clerkly discussion had already been commented on by the Pardoner and the Friar. Next, the Merchant lets Justinus quote some of the Wife's very words—though without naming her: 'God may apply the trials of marriage, my dear January, to your salvation. Your wife may make you go straight to heaven without passing through purgatory.'

> 'Paraunter she may be your purgatorie!
> She may be Goddes mene, and Goddes whippe;
> Than shal your soule up, to hovene skippe
> Swifter than doth an arwe out of the bowe.'

This is merely an adaptation of the Wife, of Bath's own language in speaking of her fourth husband:

> 'By God, in erthe I was his purgatorie,
> For which I hope his soule be in glorie.'

Compare also another phrase of hers, which Justinus echoes: 'Myself have been the whippe.' And finally, when all the Pilgrims are quite prepared for such a thing, there is a frank citation of the Wife of Bath by name, with a reference to her exposition of marriage:

> 'My tale is doon:—for my wit is thinne.
> Beth not agast herof, my brother dere.
> *But lat us waden out of this matere:*
> *The Wyf of Bathe, if ye han understande,*
> *Of marriage, which we have on honde,*
> *Declared hath ful wel in litel space.*
> Fareth now wel, God have yow in his grace.'

Are the italicized lines a part of the speech of Justinus, or are they interpolated by the Merchant, in his own person, in order to shorten Justinus' harangue? Here is Professor Skeat's comment: 'These four parenthetical lines interrupt the story rather awkwardly. They obviously belong to the narrator, the Merchant, as it is out of the question that Justinus had heard of the Wife of Bath. Perhaps it is an oversight! Now it makes no difference whether we assign these lines to Justinus or to the Merchant, for Justinus, as we have seen, has immediately before quoted the Wife s very words, and he may as well mention her as repeat her language. Either way, the lines are exquisitely in place. *Chaucer* is not speaking, and there is no violation of dramatic propriety on his part. It is not Chaucer who is telling the story. It is the Merchant. And the Merchant is telling it as a part of the discussion which the Wife has started. It is dramatically proper, then, that the Merchant should quote the Wife of Bath and that he should refer to her. And it is equally proper, from the dramatic point of view, for Chaucer to let the Merchant make Justinus mention the Wife. In that case it is the Merchant—not *Chaucer*—who chooses to have one of his characters fall out of his part for a moment and make a 'local allusion.' Chaucer is responsible for making the *Merchant* speak in character; the Merchant, in his turn, is responsible for *Justinus*. That the Merchant should put into the mouth of Justinus a remark that Justinus could never have made is, then, not a slip on Chaucer's part. On the contrary, it is a first-rate dramatic touch, for it is precisely what the Merchant might well have done under the circumstances.

Nor should we forget the exquisitely comical discussion between Pluto and Proserpina which the Merchant has introduced near the end of his story. This dialogue is a flagrant violation of dramatic propriety—not on Chaucer's part, however, but on the Merchant's. And therein consists a portion of its merit. For the Merchant is so eager to make his point that he rises superior to all artistic rules. He is bent, not on giving utterance to a masterpiece of narrative construction, but on enforcing his lesson in every possible way. And Chaucer is equally bent on making him do it. Hence the Queen of the Lower World is brought in, discoursing in terms that befit the Wife of Bath (the presiding genius of this part of the *Canterbury Tales*), and echoing some of her very doctrines. And note that Pluto (who is as fond of citing authorities as the Wife's last husband) yields the palm of the discussion to Proserpine. This, too, was the experience of the Wife's husbands. The tone and manner of the whole debate between Pluto and his queen are wildly absurd if regarded from the point of view of gods and goddesses, but in that very incongruity resides their dramatic propriety. What we have is not Pluto and Proserpine arguing with each other, but the Wife of Bath and one of her husbands attired for the nonce by the cynical Merchant in the external resemblance of King Pluto and his dame.

The end of the Merchant's Tale does not bring the Marriage Chapter of the *Canterbury Tales* to a conclusion. As the Merchant had commented on the Clerk's Tale by speaking of his own wife, thus continuing the subject which the Wife had begun, so the Host comments on the Merchant's story by making a similar application:

'Ey, Goddes mercy,' seyde our Hoste tho,
'Now such a wyf I pray God kepe me fro!'

'See how women deceive us poor men, as the Merchant has shown us. However, my wife is true as any steel; but she is a shrew, and has plenty of other faults.' And just as the Merchant had referred expressly to the Wife of Bath, so also does the Host refer to her expressly: 'But I must not talk of these things. If I should, it would be told to her by some of this company. I need not say by whom, 'sin wommen connen outen swich chaffare!' Of course the Host points this remark by looking at the Wife of Bath. There are but three women in the company. Neither the highborn and dainty Prioress nor the pious nun who accompanies her is likely to gossip with Harry Baily's spouse. It is the Wife, a woman of the

Hostess's own rank and temper, who will tattle when the party returns to the Tabard. And so we find the Wife of Bath still in the foreground, as she has been, in one way or another, for several thousand lines.

But now the Host thinks his companions have surely had enough of marriage. It is time they heard something of love, and with this in view he turns abruptly to the Squire, whom all the Pilgrims have come to know as 'a lovyer and a lusty bachiller.'

> 'Quier, com neer, if it your wille be,
> And sey somewhat of *love*; for certes ye
> Connen theron as muche as any man.'

The significance of the emphasis on *love*, which is inevitable if the address to the Squire is read (as it should be) continuously with the Host's comments on marriage, is by no means accidental.

There is no psychology about the Squire's Tale,—no moral or social or matrimonial theorizing. It is pure romance, in the mediaeval sense. The Host understood the charm of variety. He did not mean to let the discussion drain itself to the dregs.

But Chaucer's plan in this Act is not yet finished. There is still something lacking to a full discussion of the relations between husband and wife. We have had the wife who dominates her husband; the husband who dominates his wife; the young wife who befools her dotard January; the chaste wife who is a scold and stirs up strife. Each of these illustrates a different kind of marriage,—but there is left untouched, so far, the ideal relation, that in which love continues and neither party to the contract strives for the mastery. Let this be set forth, and the series of views of wedded life begun by the Wife of Bath will be rounded off; the Marriage Act of the Human Comedy will be concluded. The Pilgrims may not be thinking of this; but there is at least one of them (as the sequel shows) who has the idea in his head. And who is be? The only pilgrims who have not yet already told their tales are the yeoman, two priests, the five tradesmen (haberdasher, carpenter, weaver, dyer, and tapicer), the parson, the plowman, the manciple, and the franklin. Of all these there is but one to whom a tale illustrating the ideal would not be inappropriate—the Franklin. To him, then, must Chaucer assign it, or leave the debate unfinished.

At this point, the dramatic action and interplay of characters are beyond all praise. The Franklin is not brought forward in formal fashion to address the company. His summons is incidental to the dialogue. No sooner has the Squire ended his chivalric romance, than the Franklin begins to compliment him:

> 'In feyth, squier, thou hast thee well yquit
> And gentilly....'

'You have acquitted yourself well and *like a gentleman*!' *Gentilesse*, then, is what has most impressed the Franklin in the tale that he has just heard. And the reason for his enthusiasm soon appears. He is, as we know, a rich freeholder, often sheriff in his county. Socially, he is not quite within the pale of the gentry, but he is the kind of man that may hope to found a family, the kind of man from whose ranks the English nobility has been constantly recruited. And that such is his ambition comes out naïvely and with a certain pathos in what he goes on to say: 'I wish my son were like you.' It is the contrast between the Squire and his own son, in whom his hopes are centered, that has led the Franklin's thoughts to *gentilesse*, a subject which is ever in his mind.

But the Host interrupts him rudely: 'Straw for your gentilesse! It is your turn to entertain the company':

> 'Telle on thy tale withouten wordes mo!'

The Franklin is, of course, very polite in his reply to this rough and unexpected command. Like the others, he is on his guard against opposing the Host and incurring the forfeit.

Here, then, as in the case of the Merchant, the Host has taken advantage of a spontaneous remark on some Pilgrim's part to demand a story. Yet the details of the action are quite different. On the previous occasion, the Merchant is requested to go on with an account of his marriage, since he has already begun to talk about it; and, though he declines to speak further of his own troubles, he does continue to discuss and illustrate wedlock from his own point of view. In the present instance, on the contrary, the Host repudiates the topic of *gentilesse*, about which the Franklin is discoursing to the Squire. He bids him drop the subject and tell a story. The Franklin pretends to be compliant, but after all, he has his own way. Indeed, he takes delicate vengeance on the Host by telling a tale which thrice exemplifies *gentilesse*—on the part of a knight, a squire, and a clerk. Thus he finishes his interrupted compliment to the Squire, and incidentally honors two other Pilgrims who have seemed to him to possess the quality that he values so highly. He proves, too, both that *gentilesse* is an entertaining topic and that it is not (as the Host has roughly intimated) a theme which he, the Franklin, is ill-equipped to handle.

For the Franklin's Tale is a gentleman's story, and he tells it like a gentleman. It is derived, he tells us, from 'thise olde *gentil* Britons.' Dorigen lauds Arveragus' *gentilesse* toward her in refusing to insist on soveraynetee in marriage. Aurelius is deeply impressed by the knight's *gentilesse* in allowing the lady to keep her word, and emulates it by releasing her. And finally, the clerk releases Aurelius, from the same motive of generous emulation.

Thus it appears that the dramatic impulse to the telling of the Franklin's Tale is to be found in the relations among the Pilgrims and in the effect that they have upon each other,—in other words, in the circumstances, the situation, and the interplay of character.

It has sometimes been thought that the story, either in subject or in style, is too fine for the Franklin to tell. But this objection Chaucer foresaw and forestalled. The question is not whether this tale, thus told, would be appropriate to a typical or 'average' fourteenth-century franklin. The question is whether it is appropriate to this particular Franklin, under these particular circumstances, and at this particular juncture. And to this question there can be but one answer. Chaucer's Franklin is an individual, not a mere type-specimen. He is rich, ambitious socially, and profoundly interested in the matter of *gentilesse* for personal and family reasons. He is trying to bring up his son as a gentleman, and his position as 'St. Julian in his country' has brought him into intimate association with first-rate models. He has, under the special circumstances, every motive to tell a gentleman's story and tell it like a gentleman. He is speaking under the immediate influence of his admiration for the Squire and of his sense of the inferiority of his own son. If we choose to conceive the Franklin as a mediaeval Squire Western and then to allege that he could not possibly have told such a story, we are making the difficulty for ourselves. We are considering—not Chaucer's Franklin (whose character is to be inferred not merely from the description in the General Prologue but from all the other evidence that the poet provides)—not Chaucer's Franklin, but somebody quite different, somebody for whom Chaucer has no kind of responsibility.

In considering the immediate occasion of the Franklin's Tale, we have lost sight for a moment of the Wife of Bath. But she was not absent from the mind of the Franklin. The proper subject of his tale, as we have seen, is *gentilesse*. Now that (as well as marriage) was a subject on which the Wife of Bath had descanted at some length. Her views are contained in the famous harangue delivered by the lady to her husband on the wedding night: 'But for ye speken of swich gentilesse,' etc. Many readers have perceived that this portentous curtain-lecture clogs the story, and some have perhaps wished it away, good as it is in itself. For it certainly seems to be out of place on the lips of the *fée*. But its insertion is (as usual in such cases) exquisitely appropriate to the teller of the tale, the Wife of Bath, who cannot help dilating on subjects which interest her, and who has had the advantage of learned society in the person of her fifth husband. Perhaps no *fée* would have talked thus to her knightly bridegroom on such an occasion; but it is quite in character for the Wife of Bath to use the *fée* (or anybody else) as a mouthpiece for her own ideas, as the Merchant had used Proserpine to point his satire. Thus the references to Dante, Valerius, Seneca, Boethius, and Juvenal—so deliciously absurd on the lips of a *fée* of King Arthur's time—are perfectly in place when we remember who it is that is reporting the monologue. The Wife was a citer of authorities—she makes the *fée* cite authorities. How comical this is the Wife did not know, but Chaucer knew, and if we think he did not, it is our own fault for not observing how dramatic in spirit is the *Canterbury Tales*.

A considerable passage in the curtain-lecture is given to the proposition that 'swich gentilesse as is descended out of old richesse' is of no value: 'Swich arrogance is not worth an hen.' These sentiments the Franklin echoes:

> 'Fy on possessioun
> But-if a man be vertuous withal!'

But, whether or not the Wife's digression on *gentilesse* is lingering in the Franklin's mind (as I am sure it is), one thing is perfectly clear: the Franklin's utterances on marriage are spoken under the influence of the discussion which the Wife has precipitated. In other words, though everybody else imagines that the subject has been finally dismissed by the Host when he calls on the Squire for a tale of *love*, it has no more been dismissed in fact than when the Friar attempted to dismiss it at the beginning of his tale. For the Franklin has views, and he means to set them forth. He possesses, as he thinks, the true solution of the whole difficult problem. And that solution he embodies in his tale of *gentilesse*.

The introductory part of the Franklin's Tale sets forth a theory of the marriage relation quite different from anything that has so far emerged in the debate. And this theory the Franklin arrives at by taking into consideration both *love* (which, as we remember, was the subject that the Host had bidden the Squire treat of) and *gentilesse* (which is to be the subject of his own story).

Arveragus had of course been obedient to his lady during the period of courtship, for obedience was well understood to be the duty of a lover. Finally, she consented to marry him—

> To take him for hir houbonde and hir lord,
> Of swich lordshipe as men han over her wyves.

Marriage, then, according to the orthodox doctrine (as held by Walter and Griselda) was to change Arveragus from the lady's servant to her master. But Arveragus was an enlightened and chivalric gentleman, and be promised the lady he would never assert his marital authority, but would content himself with the mere name of sovereignty, continuing to be her servant and lover as before. This be did because be thought it would ensure the happiness of their wedded life.

But, just as Arveragus was no disciple of the Marquis Walter, so Dorigen was not a member of the sect of the Wife of Bath. She promised her husband obedience and fidelity in return for his *gentilesse* in renouncing his sovereign rights. This, then, is the Franklin's solution of the whole puzzle of matrimony, and it is a solution that depends upon love and *gentilesse* on both sides. But he is not content to leave the matter in this purely objective condition. He is determined that there shall be no misapprehension in the mind of any Pilgrim as to his purpose. He wishes to make it perfectly clear that he is definitely and formally offering this theory as the only satisfactory basis of happy married life. And he accordingly comments on the relations between the married lovers with fulness, and with manifest reference to certain things that the previous debaters have said.

The arrangement, he tells the Pilgrims, resulted in 'quiet and rest' for both Arveragus and Dorigen. And, he adds, it is the only arrangement which will ever enable two persons to live together in love and amity. Friends must 'obey each other if they wish to hold company long.' Hence it was that this wise knight promised his wife 'suffraunce' and that she promised him never to abuse his goodness. The result, the Franklin adds, was all that could be desired. The knight lived 'in blisse and in solas.' And then the Franklin adds an encomium on the happiness of true marriage:

> 'Who coulde telle, but he had wedded be,
> The ioye, the ese, and the prosperitee
> That is bitwixe an housbonde and his wyf?'

This encomium echoes the language of the Merchant:

> 'A wyf! a Seinte Marie! *benedicte*!
> How mighte a man han any adversitee
> That hath a wyf? Certes, I can nat seye!
> The blisse which that is bitwixe hem tweye
> Ther may no tonge telle or herte thinke!

The Franklin's praise of marriage is sincere; the Merchant's had been savagely ironical. The Franklin, we observe, is answering the Merchant, and he answers him in the most effective way—by repeating his very words.

And just as in the Merchant's Tale we noted that the Merchant has enormously expanded the simple *fabliau* that he had to tell, inserting all manner of observations on marriage which are found in no other version of the Pear-Tree story, so also we find that the Franklin's exposition of the ideal marriage relation (including the pact between Arveragus and Dorigen) is all his own, occurring in none of the versions that precede Chaucer. These facts are of the very last significance. No argument is necessary to enforce their meaning.

It is hardly worth while to indicate the close connection between this and that detail of the Franklin's exposition and certain points that have come out in the discussion as conducted by his predecessors in the debate. His repudiation of the Wife of Bath's doctrine that men should be 'governed by their wives' is express, as well as his rejection of the opposite theory. Neither party should lose his liberty; neither the husband nor the wife should be a thrall. Patience (which clerks celebrate as a high virtue) should be mutual, not, as in the Clerk's Tale, all on one

side. The husband is to be both servant and lord—servant in love and
lord in marriage. Such servitude is true lordship. Here there is a manifest
allusion to the words of Walter's subjects in the Clerk's Tale:

> That blisful yok
> Of sovereynetee, noght of servyse;

as well as to Walter's rejoinder:

> 'I me reioysed of my libertee,
> That selde tyme is founde in mariage;
> Ther I was free, I moot been in servage.'

It was the regular theory of the Middle Ages that the highest type of
chivalric love was incompatible with marriage, since marriage brings in
mastery, and mastery and love cannot abide together. This view the
Franklin boldly challenges. Love *can* be consistent with marriage, he
declares. Indeed, without love (and perfect *gentle* love) marriage is sure
to be a failure. The difficulty about mastery vanishes when mutual love
and forbearance are made the guiding principles of the relation between
husband and wife.

The soundness of the Franklin's theory, he declares, is proved by
his tale. For the marriage of Arveragus and Dorigen was a brilliant
success. Thus the whole debate has been brought to a satisfactory
conclusion, and the Marriage Act of the Human Comedy ends with the
conclusion of the Franklin's Tale.

Those readers who are eager to know what Chaucer thought about
marriage may feel reasonably content with the inference that may be
drawn from his procedure. The Marriage Group of Tales begins with the
Wife of Bath's Prologue and ends with the Franklin's Tale. There is no
connection between the Wife's Prologue and the group of stories that
precedes: there is no connection between the Franklin's Tale and the
group that follows. Within the Marriage Group, on the contrary, there
is close connection throughout. That act is a finished act. It begins and
ends an elaborate debate. We need not hesitate, therefore, to accept the
solution which the Franklin offers as that which Geoffrey Chaucer the
man accepted for his own part. Certainly it is a solution that does him
infinite credit. A better has never been devised or imagined.

LARRY D. BENSON

The Beginnings of Chaucer's
English Style

By "the beginnings of Chaucer's English style" I mean how Chaucer began to write in English and how he learned to do so to such marvelous effect that even in his first important work, *The Book of the Duchess*, he is in full control of what we easily recognize as the true Chaucerian style. That is the first work we can date with any degree of confidence— around 1370—and by then Chaucer had an easy command of the English poetic line. The beginnings of this—Chaucer's first attempts at verse—must have come long before this, how long we can only guess.

Since it is always best to be as specific as possible when you are only guessing anyway, I put that in the year 1357, when Chaucer was somewhere between 14 and 17 years old and first appears in the records of a royal court, in the household of the countess of Ulster, wife to Prince Lionel. It must have been a good year for Chaucer—he was a young courtier, with all the world before him, in the most magnificent court in Europe, still flushed with its victory at Poitiers. It is also a very good time for me, since it is a very lightly documented part of Chaucer's life, with no surviving texts to get in the way of my theories.

Of course, Chaucer must have known about English poetry long before he began to write it. The London in which he was born and passed his childhood years was already a lively center of a rapidly growing English literary culture. The Auchinleck Manuscript, written in

London about the time of Chaucer's birth, is a good index to that culture. It is an impressive manuscript, very large (over 330 folios), well written, and with a number of miniature illustrations. It must therefore have been quite expensive, intended perhaps for some prosperous London merchant—someone like Chaucer's own prosperous merchant-father. It is an anthology of saints' lives, miracles, chronicles, and romances—all in English. It was, to quote Derek Pearsall, written for an audience that "relished familiar piety and instruction" but that "desired access, in its native tongue, to the historical dignities and fashionable *haut monde* of [French] romance."[1] It has been argued that Chaucer knew this very manuscript—or one just like it—since the romances in the Auchinleck are the very ones he satirizes in *Sir Thopas*.[2] That mockery, I believe, is affectionate, and it is at once so gentle and so detailed that it argues for his long acquaintance with and careful reading of works of this genre.

The same should be said of Chaucer's taste for "familiar piety"—for brief saints' lives, miracles of the Virgin, and tales of virtuous suffering. Chaucer is unusual among sophisticated poets of the time in that he wrote not only learned works of piety and instruction—such as the *Melibee* and the *Parson's Tale*—but works of popular devotion, such as the Second Nun's *Life of St. Cecelia* and the *Prioress's Tale*. The latter comes close to what some critics call "bad art," and one student of Chaucer's style muses on the mystery of why it is that one can find so many relations of Chaucer's work to the "bad art" of the time and so few to the good—the work of the *Gawain*-poet or even Gower.[3] The answer is simple enough; they weren't around when Chaucer was a boy, and "bad art"—we should rather say "popular art," for much of it is pretty good—is all there was. Chaucer must have read such poems—and heard others, songs and lays—read or sung aloud throughout his boyhood years, for his enduring love of English verse—even that which modern critics think bad—argues for an early and intimate acquaintance with the English literary culture of the London of his childhood years.

However, the court in which Chaucer served in 1357, where he spent his formative years and with which his future was inextricably bound, remained officially French in language and literary culture. Unofficially it was bilingual. Though nineteenth-century historians thought Edward III could barely speak his native tongue, Edward certainly knew English and may even have enjoyed some English poetry; he was fond of using English chivalric mottoes such as "syker as the wode bynd," and at least once he even used a bit of English verse for his *impressa*.[4] Nevertheless, the official literature of his court—this at a time when literature had become an essential part of court life—was purely French. Jean Froissart, whose dream visions Chaucer greatly admired, was a member of Edward's court, serving as the queen's secretary, and there were other poets as well, including Sir Oton de Graunson, whom Chaucer later called "flower of hem that make in France."

Oton de Graunson may have been the editor of a collection of lyric poetry, compiled in the late 1350s or early 1360s in or for the English court and preserved in a manuscript now at the University of Pennsylvania (MS 15).[5] The manuscript contains 310 poems—all courtly, secular works in the elegant forms so widely cultivated at the time, and, of course, all in French. They are all contemporary poems—*ballades*, *rondeaux*, and *chants royeaux* by Machaut, Froissart, Oton de Graunson, Jean de la Mote, Philippe de Vitry, and other fashionable poets of the day. A good many of these poems were well known to Chaucer and are echoed in such early works as *The Book of the Duchess*.[6] Indeed, the version in this manuscript of Oton de Graunson's sequence of *ballades*, which Chaucer translated in 'The Complaint of Venus," is closer to that which Chaucer used than any other surviving version.[7] Chaucer may not have known this manuscript itself, but he certainly knew one very similar to it.

Along with the works of poets such as Oton de Graunson, Machaut, and Froissart, the Pennsylvania manuscript also includes a number of poems labelled with the initials "Ch." Some years ago Rossell H. Robbins made a good argument for the case that Geoffrey Chaucer, at least in his youth, was actually "Geffroi Chaucier, poete français."[8] Robbins may well be right, and it is tempting to think that the poems labelled "Ch" in the Pennsylvania manuscript are indeed the work of the young "Geffroi Chaucier." I wish they were, because some of them are pretty good, but James Wimsatt, the editor of the poems of "Ch," resists the temptation of flatly claiming them for Chaucer, and I follow his good example.

But in a way that is beside the point. Whether or not Chaucer was the author of these poems, they are the kind of poetry that he and his friends read when he was reaching early manhood in the royal court. They are fashionable, courtly, polished, highly allegorical, filled with allusions to classical and courtly mythology, and written in the demanding fixed forms of fourteenth-century French poetry. They exemplify the sort of poetry that was read and admired in the royal court, providing patterns of thought and language for young gentlemen who vied to see who could "speak most feelingly of love." They are, in short, the kind of poems that defined what sophisticated poetry was for the young Geoffrey Chaucer. Wimsatt, in his edition, slyly inserts this capsule biography of "Ch":

> He entered the royal court around 1357, at the age of 14, where he often heard French poetry read and sung; "Ch" soon tried his own skill in the fashionable modes of court verse. It was of course French verse, French having been the vernacular of court literature in England for centuries. The courtiers wrote their poetry in French, and it did not occur to a beginner like "Ch" to do otherwise.[9]

It is hard not to substitute "Chaucer" for "Ch," and I am sure that is what Wimsatt intended. It is a plausible account of the beginning of Chaucer's poetic career, and I have no doubt that, as Robbins argued and Wimsatt broadly hints, Chaucer did indeed write some of his first poems in French, and that those poems were very similar to those of "Ch."

Yet, despite the pressure of precedent in favor of French and despite the very strong probability that many of his early poems were written in French, young Geoffrey Chaucer also chose very early on to write in English, and by the time of *The Book of the Duchess*, around 1370, English was his chosen medium for his most important works. One is tempted to speculate about the reasons why Chaucer chose to write in English in a court whose official culture was French and the question of just who in that court would have wanted to listen to his English poems. It would be fun, but finally it would come down to a matter of generations (it is notable that Chaucer's earliest poems are associated with people roughly his own age), to the fact that Chaucer genuinely loved the English language, and to the pressure of the historical forces that brought English back into prominence in Chaucer's lifetime. By 1357 there were already many—probably most—of the gentle classes who spoke French badly if at all. Other young men of the time— Langland, the *Gawain*-poet, perhaps even Gower—must also have been taking up English verse at this time, and Chaucer's first major poems are not far in time from what amounted to a great flowering of English literature throughout the land.

But before Chaucer could write English poetry he had to find an English poetic language and style. For that he had to begin with what English had to offer. Poets of any time must begin by writing poetry of the sort they have read or heard; that is what defines poetry for them. One must start with what the tradition offers. Of course, in the Middle Ages the tradition had aesthetic value in itself. Those nineteenth-century critics who prized "originality" and dismissed so much fourteenth-century French poetry as merely derivative and "conventional" missed the point. The derivative and therefore conventional elements of the verse—the echoes of the previous tradition in the repetition of a fixed set of words, formulae, gestures, and actions—served to invoke the tradition and thus to appropriate for the individual poem its "aesthetic funding," by which I mean the associations—poetic and social—that words, phrases, even meters and stanzaic forms acquired from their repeated uses over the years.[10]

Chaucer's problem—it epitomizes the problem that faced English literature in general at the time—was that he had two traditions of poetry, two definitions of what it should be. The English tradition that rang in his ears from early childhood—which he obviously relished— carried a set of associations completely different from those of the French, which defined—even for English speakers—what civilized, courtly poetry should be. To write in English for an audience of fellow courtiers steeped in the French tradition Chaucer had to find a way to evoke the courtly style of French poetry in his own English verse.

This had never been done successfully, though it had been tried a number of times since the beginning of the fourteenth century. English verse in the thirteenth century is often of a very high quality—one need only think of *The Owl and the Nightingale*, and there may have been other masterpieces that have since been lost. Moreover, in the thirteenth century there had developed a solid and workmanlike poetic line—the four-beat English couplet, which was a plain, straightforward style suitable not only for simple romances such as *Floris and Blancheflour* but for chronicles, for saints' lives, and for works of instruction and edification. It was a useful, flexible, and potentially forceful style. It was not an elegant form of verse, not highly decorative; it was simple and direct. The thirteenth century—in French as well as English—was, compared with the fourteenth, relatively restrained and plain in its artistic tastes.

The finest achievement of English thirteenth-century verse is the lyric parallel to this plain narrative style, the simple English songs celebrating the seasons, such as the famous "Somer is icumen in," or expressing the joys and sorrows of love, such as "My lief is faren in lond." Chaucer knew the latter; it is the song that Chauntecleer and Pertelote sing in *The Nun's Priest's Tale*.[11] Chaucer quotes only the first line, expecting his audience to know the rest. Here is the whole poem:

> My lief is faren in londe
> Allas! Why is she so?
> And I am so sore bound
> I may nat com her to.
> She hath my hert in hold,
> Wherever I ride or go,
> With trewe love a thousand fold.[12]

Chaucer may later have thought this a bit naive. He presents it as a song sung by a couple of chickens, and certainly the last three lines sound a bit weak—perhaps because we do not have the music.

The music, of course, is very important. These early lyrics were sung—sometimes, as in the case of "Somer is icumen in," in quite complicated fashions. With the words alone we have only the basic framework of the piece. Nevertheless, the characteristics of the verbal style are clear. The vocabulary is completely native, composed entirely of English words. *Allas* is ultimately from the Old French *Helas*, but it had been in the language for over two hundred years and had been completely naturalized by the time this author used it. The syntax is straightforward: regular, declarative, almost prosaic in structure. And there is no obvious ornamentation, with only the slightest touch of alliteration in "lief ... in londe" and "hert in hold," just enough to add fluidity to the statement, invoking only a touch of the associations of the older alliterative tradition. What poetic force this little lyric has derives from a direct, though polished, simplicity of statement.

As I have said, Chaucer's first poetic attempts may very well have been in French, and we have in the poems of "Ch" examples of what they may have been like—exercises, that is, in the dominant style of French secular lyric. But I suspect that about the same time he was also making his first attempts at English verse, exercises in what was then the dominant style of English secular poetry, that of the simple declarative lyric exemplified by "My lief is faren in londe." There are a number of them embedded in Chaucer's earlier works—in *The Book of the Duchess*, *The House of Fame*, and *The Knight's Tale*. There are two of them in *The Book of the Duchess*. The first is the song that the Man in Black recites to himself, as yet unaware of the dreamer's presence:

> I have of sorwe so greet won   475
> That joye get I never none
> Now that I se my lady bright,
> Which I have loved with al my might,
> Is fro me ded and is agoon.
> Allas, deth, what ayleth the,   480
> That thou noldest have taken me,
> When thou took my lady sweet,
> That was so fair, so fresh, so fre,
> So good that men may wel se,
> Of al goodnesse she had no mete!   485

Ezra Pound was especially fond of this poem, which he printed in his very brief section on Chaucer in his *ABC of Reading*. Though Chaucer specified that the poem was recited rather than sung (in keeping with what was then the new fashion in French verse), Pound was clearly right when he wrote in his usual telegraphic style:

> Idiom has changed, but no greater fitness to be sung has been attained, not even by Shakespeare with the aid of later Italian song-books.[13]

Pound could just as well have taken the second lyric recited by the Man in Black, the one that he says that he wrote to express his first love for Blanche:

> Lord, hyt maketh myn herte lyght   1175
> Whan I thenke on that swete wyght
> That is so semely on to see;
> And wisshe to God hit myghte so bee
> That she wolde holde me for hir knyght,
> My lady, that is so fair and bryght!   1180

These lyrics are pure English; together they have but two words of French derivation—"allas" and "joy." "Joy," like "allas," was an ultimately French word, completely naturalized after over two centuries of use in English. The style of these lyrics embodies the simple diction, straightforward syntax, and the lightly alliterating ornamentation ("so fair, so fresh, so fre") of the straightforward declarative style of thirteenth- and early fourteenth-century English lyric.

It was perhaps only a happy accident that the simple style of the English lyric of the time so closely resembled the simple French lyric of the thirteenth century. French songs, such as the simple *reverdi*, the celebration of the return of spring and love, and many of the even earlier Provençal lyrics appealed to Ezra Pound because of their economy of statement, their directness of language and syntax and lack of ornamentation. He admired the lyrics in *The Book of the Duchess* not for the English qualities that I have stressed but because he thought Chaucer had so clearly caught the true spirit of Provençal song.[14]

I am not sure if Pound's reading is right or wrong. But I think that is the way Chaucer's first audience read or heard these simple songs. Their literary taste, as well as Chaucer's, was shaped by the literary culture reflected in the Pennsylvania manuscript. The simple, polished style of these poems, the fact that they were written to be spoken rather than sung, in keeping with the latest fashion in French verse,[15] rendered these verses acceptable, and enjoyable, to an English-speaking audience steeped in the French tradition. These were the native equivalents of the *virelais* and *rondeaux* they knew so well.

Nevertheless, though the tradition of simple song continued in French, now in ever more elaborated forms, the dominant French lyric style of Chaucer's time was the heavier, sometimes ponderous, style of the *ballades* and "complaints" popularized by Guillaume de Machaut. Such lyrics are far and away the preponderant form in the Pennsylvania manuscript. The poems of "Ch" include only one simple song, a *virelai*; the rest are highly ornate *ballades* and *chants royeaux*, like the great majority of Chaucer's own surviving lyrics.

French poems in this style—lyrics such as the *ballades* and narratives such as the dream vision—depend not on simple, direct statement such as Chaucer knew from the English lyric but on an often elaborate, rhetorically heightened, and self-consciously courtly style. In painting, architecture, even language and manners as well as poetry, the fourteenth century was a time that prized elaboration. Court life became far more formalized, painting ever brighter and richer, and architecture more flamboyant, with a wealth of decorative detail that makes the earlier Gothic seem comparatively sober. The fork, the handkerchief, and the English plural pronoun of address are all fourteenth-century inventions.[16] The plain style of the thirteenth-century four-beat English line hardly answered to the demands of this new desire for the elegant and the ornate.

Moreover, the courtly style of verse, for narrative dream vision and romance as well as for lyric, depended on a well-understood courtly style of speech, a class dialect of the sort that had not yet developed in England, where until the fourteenth century the distinction between upper- and lower-class styles of speech depended on a difference in language rather than register.[17] Scott overdoes it in *Ivanhoe*, but in general he has it right: in the twelfth and much of the thirteenth centuries gentlemen spoke French and peasants spoke English. French served as the marker of upper-class speech; there was no need to develop a style of English speech suitable for aristocratic discourse, and there was thus no style of English speech suitable for aristocratic literature.

More precisely, there was no suitable style of London speech. The most sophisticated and ornate style in early fourteenth-century English was that of the alliterative revival. Chaucer certainly knew alliterative verse; he knew it well enough to compose perfect alliterative lines, and when he did so in *The Legend of Good Women*, he even included a touch of alliterative poetic diction.[18] But the king's court rather than the provincial courts determined the prestige dialect in literature and speech, and when aristocrats at the royal court began to speak English, they spoke London English, a fact which practically disqualified provincial stylistic models, however sophisticated.[19] Certainly alliterative verse was written in London—most notably *Piers Plowman*, but that is a poem that is determinedly uncourtly, perhaps even anti-courtly.

The only elaborate and thus potentially courtly style that London offered at the time was that of the stanzaic, or tail rhyme romances, so richly represented in the Auchinleck Manuscript. The authors of these fourteenth-century romances, responding to the new demand for elegance and ornamentation, built upon the plain style of earlier romances such as *King Horn* and *Havelok the Dane* by turning to the only elaborate style they knew (Latin, the source of French ornamentation, being largely unknown to them), the alliterative tradition. They adopted its formulaic style and developed their own set of formulas ("stif in stour," "bright in bour," etc.) and stock rhymes and fillers (such as "iwis" and "soth to tell"). They thus created a recognizable style associated with the knightly—if not aristocratic—life, insofar as they knew it. This offered at least the potential of an English style that might be used to create the English equivalent of the ornate style of the French *ballade* or even dream vision.

This had been tried a few years before Chaucer began to write by the authors of the English poems in the famous Harley Manuscript.[20] Chaucer certainly knew the romances in the Auchinleck Manuscript and there is at least a chance that he may have known that manuscript itself. There is no reason to think that he knew the Harley Manuscript itself, but he did know some of the poems it contained; he makes use of one of them, "The Fair Maid of Ribbesdale," in the *Miller's Tale*.[21]

The English Harley lyrics show an altogether new development in English literature. They are the native equivalent of the *ballades* and *chansons* now fashionable in French, and they are among the first poems in English to embody the conventions of courtly love. In other words, their authors aimed to create a style to replace the simple English song, like "My lief is faren in londe," with an elaborate English style attuned to the new taste for the ornate. Here is the first stanza of the poem usually called "Alysoun:"[22]

> Betwene Mersh and Averil
> When spray beginneth to springe
> The litel foul hath hire wil
> On hire lud to singe. ('language')
> Ich libbe in love longinge
> For semlokest of alle thinge, ('seemliest')
> He may me blisse bring;
> Ich am in hire bandoun. ('power, control')
> An hendy hap ichabbe y hent ('good fortune'; 'I have received')
> Ichot from hevene it is me sent! ('I know')
> From alle wimmen my love is lent ('taken away')
> And light on Alysoun.

The spring setting and singing birds evoke the *plaisance* of the standard French lyric. And the subject is the joys and sorrows of unrequited love. It is an elaborate French lyric recreated in English. The diction of the

English tradition remains unchanged. Except for the names of the months and that of the lady, Alysoun, there is only one French word in the entire poem—"bandoun," which had been in the language since the twelfth century. "Langeur" becomes "love longing," "cortois" "hendy," "ma dame" "my lemman."

To effect this translation, the authors of the Harley lyrics drew on the style of the only model of literature concerned with aristocratic manners that was available to them, that of the English romance. The authors of the stanzaic romances drew on the vocabulary and formulae of the alliterative tradition to elaborate the old and plain style of earlier romances such as *King Horn* or *Floris and Blancheflour*. The authors of the Harley lyrics did much the same—they drew on contemporary English romances for their stylistic elaboration. They took over the alliterative formulae—"springes the spray," "bright in bour"—the riming tags, and the vocabulary of the stanzaic romances, capitalizing upon such aristocratic associations as they had. That is to say, the language of the romances provided a kind of aesthetic funding for these lyrics. To say that a "hende knight," "stiff in stour," pleaded with his "levedy" for "lemman, thin or" was to lend the love lyric the aura of the romance, to place it firmly in the world of the aristocracy insofar as that world existed in written English.

Chaucer did somewhat the same in his first surviving attempt at narrative—Fragment A of the *Romaunt of the Rose*, which shows how deeply the English romances affected his early style. This is the more remarkable, given the fact that the *Romaunt* is a very close, line-for-line, almost word-for-word, translation. Nevertheless, the language is often reminiscent of the popular romances—in words, such as "lemman," "hende," "gent," and in phrases, such as "bright in bour," "stif in stour," "maid of pris." The lines have some of the movement and sound of the popular style, with frequent riming tags (such as "iwis," "sooth to seyn") and a heavy use of intensifiers (such as "ful" and "right"). Most important, there is a heavy use of expletives ("lo," "Lord"), asseverations ("so as I gesse," "as I trowe"), and occasional direct address to the audience ("trusteth wel," "as I shal yow say"). There is not a great deal of this direct address, but what there is draws on one of the most notable characteristics of the popular romance, the intrusive narrator.

Such a narrator is, of course, not new in medieval poetry. The narrator in the Latin rhetorical tradition is often heavily intrusive, calling attention to the act of narration in his sometimes ponderous uses of such devices as *occupatio*, of which Chaucer himself was very fond and which is frequent in the French courtly style as well. In the Latin tradition such intrusions establish the narrator not as a familiar presence but as an authority, a "rhetor" expounding from his lectern. In the French tradition the narrator is a much more lively presence—the *Roman de la rose* itself is a good example, with its sometimes conversational tone of one gentleman speaking directly and informally to another.

The narrator of the English popular romance adopts a different stance—aiming to establish not so much his authority or his status as a gentleman as to establish an intimate relation to his audience. Not an equal relationship, for the English romancer tends to show his awareness of his (real or assumed) lowly status in relation to the "lordinges" he addresses. There is an often naive but ingratiating tone to his calls for silence, remarks on his story, reassurances of the truth of his narrative, and comments on the act of narration. The stance is that of a minstrel rather than a learned rhetor or gentlemanly lover.

One finds this in French romance as well, in the contrast between the popular (perhaps "naive" is a better word) and the sophisticated romances between Beroul's *Tristan*, in which the narrator is constantly intruding to comment on his story (mainly berating his villains) and the *Tristan* of Thomas of Brittainy, whose narrator maintains a gentlemanly reserve. Guillaume de Lorris writes in a similarly reserved manner. Yet, even in closely translating Guillaume's work, Chaucer sometimes speaks directly to us in the voice of an English romancer. In the opening lines, where Guillaume has "Quar endroit moie ai ge fiance," "As for me I am sure," Chaucer has "This trowe I, and say for me" (RomA 15). The translation is exact, but the formulaic "trowe I," the repetitions, "say for me," with the rhyme on "me" and the consequent foregrounding of the narrative first person carry the voice of an English romance narrator. It is in embryo the voice that Chaucer would later develop into his own, that which allowed him to establish the complex interrelationship of narrator, reader, and narration that characterizes his later work.

The most obvious elements of the English romance style in the *Romaunt*—words such as "lemman," "hende," "druerie," and phrases such as "of pris," "bright in bour"—recur in Chaucer's later work only in comic contexts. In his celebrated study of the "Idiom of Popular Poetry in The Miller's Tale" (with popular poetry defined by the Harley Lyrics), E. T. Donaldson demonstrated that by the time Chaucer wrote the

Canterbury Tales such words had come to sound unmistakably provincial and old-fashioned to his ear.[23] In *The Miller's Tale* Chaucer uses the diction of popular romance (words and phrases he had used seriously in the *Romaunt*) to provide a satiric backdrop to the small-town dandies' attempts at courtliness—Absolon's "Ywis, lemman, I have swich love-longynge" (I.3705) and hende Nicholas' plea "For deeme love of thee, lemman, I spille" (I.3278), which he says while vigorously "thakking the likerous Alisoun about the lendes." The same style is used for the bumbling Sir Thopas, who seeks a Fairy Queen as his "lemman" and "fil in love-longynge / Al whan he herde the thrustel synge" (VII.772–73).

The authors of the Harley lyrics had used this language—as did the young Chaucer—because of its association with the prestigious world of knighthood, as it had been represented in English romance. That was the problem. English romance and the Harley Lyrics themselves are, by the standards of French fourteenth-century poetry, at best rather crude. The Harley authors are more goliardic than chivalric, and they never lose sight of the object of courtship, getting the lady into bed. The lyric "De clerico et puella" starts out well enough:

> Sorewe and syke and drery mod byndeth me so faste   5
> That y wene to walke wod yef hit me lengore laste.

But it has a happy ending, spoken by the lady:

> fader, moder, and al my kun ne shal me holde so stille   35
> that y nam thyn and thou art myn, to don al thi wille.[24]

That last line could have come straight out of an English romance, in which the heroes rarely languish for love. That is the work of the ladies, like the many maids in *Sir Thopas* who "moorne for hym paramour,/ When hem were bet to slepe" (VII.743–44). Here is Josian in *Bevis of Hampton*, one of the Auchinleck romances:[25]

> "Merci," 3he seide, "3et with than   1105
> Ichavede the leuer to me lemman,
> The bodi in the scherte naked,
> Then al the gold that Crist hath meked,
> And thou wast with me do the wille!"
> "For gode," queth he, "that i do nelle!"
> 3he fel adoun and wep ri3t sore.

Bevis stoutly resists Josian's advances until they are properly married. He is, like Sir Thopas, "chaast and no lechour." Neither is King Horn, who must endure the relentless advances of maid Rymenhild, who, like many another heroine of early English romance, has very little desire to remain a maid. One sometimes finds this sort of crudity in early French courtly poetry as well. But one does not find it in fourteenth-century French courtly verse. A Josian or a Rymenhild would have caused Lamant, the lover in the *Roman de la rose*, to faint dead away.

The Harley lyrics and the popular romances they reflect may have been the victims of their own success: the more widely such poems became known to sophisticated readers—and the Harley and Auchinleck manuscripts show that this was happening—the more obvious their crudity would have appeared to an audience schooled in the works of Guillaume de Lords, Froissart, and Machaut. That is not to put them down; they are fun, and Chaucer enjoyed them. Indeed, their crudity is part of the fun; but the aesthetic funding that the diction, stanzaic forms, and conventions of love and knighthood of the popular romances acquired when they became widely known to sophisticated readers was, at best, high kitsch.

The obvious alternative was to draw on French for one's vocabulary, stanzaic forms, and conventions and thus to depend on French itself for the aesthetic funding of one's work. In short, write French in English and appropriate for one's own work the prestige of the French language and the aristocratic associations of that literature. To some extent this is what English writers had been doing throughout the thirteenth century, when English secular verse consisted largely of the importation of French matter into English. The native four-beat couplet was certainly influenced, if not formed, by French octosyllabics, and the subject matter of English romance was largely French. Even romance tales that originated in England—the so-called "matter of England" in works such as *Havelok the Dane* and *King Horn*—survive in English versions ultimately derivative from Anglo-Norman originals, and they are to this extent attempts to lend to native verse some of the prestige of the dominant French culture. This sometimes involved the borrowing of the vocabulary of French romance and thus importing the cultural prestige of the French language itself into native verse.

That technique was elaborately developed around the beginning of the fourteenth century by the London author of the romance of *Kyng Alisaundre* (another Auchinleck romance). He was translating directly from a French romance in octosyllabic couplets, and he chose for his narrative its nearest English equivalent, the old four-beat couplet. It was, as I have said, a plain, workmanlike, potentially vigorous style. That was its problem for writers of a time that was looking for more elaborate means of expression. One could elaborate the style itself by bringing into it a heavily alliterating vocabulary and the old poetic diction, as did the English romancers I have been discussing. The author of *Kyng Alisaundre* chose instead to add elaboration and apparent sophistication simply by combining this straightforward style with a heavy infusion of French.

This seems to have been a conscious undertaking. The *Alisaundre*-poet was a master of the simple English song, and he scatters such lyrics through his work as marks of major narrative divisions. They are often seasonal, as in this example:

> In time of winter alange it is: 4199
> The foules lesen her blis,
> The leues fallen of the tre,
> Rein alangeth the cuntre.
> Maidens leseth here hewe;
> Ac euer hye louieth that he trewe.[26]

This is true English lyric, without a touch of French diction. In his narrative, as opposed to these inserted lyrics, this poet builds a French structure on this simple English base. Students of the language have often remarked his very heavy use of French, with sometimes, as Bradley noted, whole passages in which "nearly every important verb, noun and adjective is French."[27] Here is one such passage, from the opening of the romance, telling how the evil magician Neptababus uses his art to defend his land:

> Of wex he made hym *popatrices*,   French
> And dude hem fi3tten myd *latrices*,   French
> And so he lerned, *ieo vous dy*,   French
> Ay to afelle his *enemy*.   1300
> With *charmes* and with *coniurisouns*   1300, 1250
> Thus he *asaied* the *regiouns*,   1300, 1300
> That hym comen to *asaile*.   1230

I have italicized the French borrowings and in the right margin I have written the earliest recorded use in English, which is usually 1300, around the year this romance was written.[28] The label "French" marks words and phrases that do not appear elsewhere in English. Earliest recorded usage is of course not earliest actual use, but it is probably fair to assume that whereas a word that is recorded much earlier, such as "asaile" (1230), had been anglicized, was perhaps even thought of as English by native speakers, those words that are relatively new to the language carried a distinct French aura. Certainly that aura is there in *popatrices* ('wax images') and *latrices* ('tablets'), which appear nowhere else in Middle English and are simply untranslated French, as is the tag "ieo vous dy." Such usages are intended to invoke the aesthetic funding of the French language and thus to raise the style of this English romance to a level closer to French romance itself. This for an audience composed, as the author says, of gentlemen who knew no French, but who, like the audience of the Auchinleck Manuscript, wanted access to "the historical dignities and *haute monde* of French Romance." The author of *Kyng Alisaundre* provided this access by making his work sound as French as possible to the ears of an English-speaking audience.

Chaucer tried this same technique, with sometimes painful results, in such early lyrics as "The ABC" or this, the second stanza of the Bill of Complaint (lines 64–70) in "The Complainte Unto Pity" (again I have marked the date of first recorded use, noting simply "First use" rather than the date when that is the case):

Hit stondeth thus: your *contraire*, *Crueltee*,	First use, 1230
Allyed is ayenst your *regalye*	First use
Under *colour* of womanly *Beaute*—	1300, 1325
For men shulde nat, lo, knowe hir *tirannye*—	First use
With *Bounte*, *Gentilesse*, and *Curtesye*,	1360, 1300, 1230
And bath *depryved* yow now of your *place*	1350, 1230
That hyghte "*Beaute apertenant* to Grace."	1325, First use, 1225

The language is almost pure French, with the multiplication of abstract allegorizations that is characteristic of the French poems in the Pennsylvania manuscript, including the poems of "Ch." It is not a style that much appeals to us, but obviously Chaucer liked it; he went on working in this heavily ornamented mode and finally, with the help of the Italian poets, found a way to turn it into poetry. But clearly so ponderous a style is far from what Wordsworth emphasized must be the basis of poetry, "the real language of men." And real language is what was needed if one was to find an English equivalent to the narrative style of Froissart or Machaut. Their tone, as I have noted, is basically that of polished and elevated conversation—one elegant gentleman speaking to another, with a delightful lightness of touch, yet with a flexibility that allows the narrator to move easily from a confiding, informal tone to ornate descriptions and elaborate allegories.

I suppose that the English writer of the time who comes closest to this style is John Gower, Chaucer's friend and fellow poet. His style owes very little to the English tradition, which he seems almost consciously to avoid. He aimed instead at what he called the "middle way," neither too near colloquial speech, on the one hand, nor too elaborately ornamental on the other. And he succeeded; his smooth and polished couplets flow with Gallic ease, perfected by long practice in composing French octosyllables.[29]

Chaucer chose another method. Almost as if in reaction to the overly Frenchified language of lyrics such as "The Complainte unto Pity," when Chaucer wrote *The Book of the Duchess* he turned to a much plainer, far more colloquial English style. It is a development of what we saw in *The Romaunt of the Rose* but now without the constraints of close translation. Derek Brewer, in his study of the opening lines of this work, has shown how heavily these lines are indebted to the popular style— most obvious in its use of expletives, asseverations, and colloquial asides:[30]

I have great wonder, be this light,	1	
How that I lyve, for day ne nyght		
I may nat slepe wel nygh noght;		
I have so many an ydel thought		
Purely for *defaut* of slep,	1297, 1290	
That, by my trouthe, I take no kep		
Of nothing, how hyt cometh or gooth,		
Ne me nys nothyng leef nor looth.		
Al is ylyche good to me—		
Joye or sorowe, wherso hyt be—	1225	10
For I have felynge in nothyng,		
But as yt were a mased thyng,		
Alway in *poynt* to falle a-doun;	1225	

> For sorwful *ymagynacioun*   1340
> Ys alway hooly in my mynde.

These lines are a close paraphrase of Froissart's *Paradis d'amours*. Indeed, *The Book of the Duchess* is Chaucer's most thoroughly French work, the centerpiece of what used to be called his "French period."

In language, however, it is Chaucer's most English work. There is not a single romance borrowing until the fifth line—"purely" and "defaut"—both of which, as the dates show, were already well at home in English. And not a single romance word has the emphasis of rime until "ymagynacioun," a recent borrowing (Chaucer's is only the second recorded usage in English) whose learned and thus elevated quality is enhanced by the simplicity of the English words with which it is surrounded. Joseph Mersand, in his still-standard work on Chaucer's *Romance Vocabulary*, remarked upon "the overwhelmingly Anglo-Saxon proportion" of the vocabulary of *The Book of the Duchess*, in which he found "that the romance words as used in the text [i.e. a dynamic analysis] are only 7.14 per cent"[31]—the lowest proportion he found in any of Chaucer's poems. The reason for this is not that Chaucer was unable to incorporate more French into his works, as Mersand implies. Chaucer was trying to create in these lines a narrative style that would reflect actual speech. And it is indeed, as Derek Brewer says, "the language as it had been spoken and evolved in the country for nearly a thousand years," and as that had been used by earlier English romances.[32]

Yet the style is also at times elaborately French, with the vocabulary of some passages as purely French as that which we saw in *Kyng Alisaundre*. When the Man in Black begins to tell the dreamer of his love, he says that since he first began to "comprehend in any thing" what love was,

> Dredeles, I have ever yit   764
> Be *tributarye* and yive *rente*   First use 1154
> To Love, hooly with good *entente*,   1225
> And through *plesaunce* become his thral   First use
> With good wille, body, hert, and al.
> Al this I putte in his *servage*,   1290
> As to my lord, and dide *homage*....   1290
>   (lines 764–70)

The language is French—the first usages underscoring that fact—and the style is French in its allegorical rendering of the surrender to love as an act of feudal allegiance. It draws directly on the aesthetic funding of aristocratic French poetry, since it not only evokes the general associations of French courtly verse but reproduces in small that scene in the *Roman de la rose* in which Lamant swears fealty to the God of Love.[33]

The Black Knight—and thus by implication John of Gaunt himself—is cast in the role of the ideal lover in French courtly verse and his language is replete with words "plesaunce," "servage," "homage" that not only might have been used by Lamant in *Le Roman de la rose*, they actually were used by him.[34] The language is, in short, the language of the perfect French gentleman, transposed into an English that real gentlemen might use, though one suspects they seldom did. Doubtless it gave John of Gaunt considerable pleasure to hear his idealized self playing the part of Lamant, the ideal lover, and speaking in this elegant, polished, highly civilized manner—speaking words which, as the God of Love says in the *Roman de la rose*, could never "issue out of a peasant's thought."[35]

But they could issue out of even an actual gentleman's thought, because of the colloquial style that Chaucer managed here to create and to maintain even in the more elaborated parts of his work. Immediately before the speech I have just quoted, there is a brief dialogue between the dreamer and the Man in Black, when the Man in Black asks the dreamer if he will listen carefully to what he says:

> "Yis, syr." "Swere thy trouthe therto,"   753
> "Gladly." "Do thanne holde hereto!"
> "I shal ryght blythely, so God me save,
> Hooly, with al the wit I have,
> Here yow as wel as I kan."
> "A goddes half!" quod he, and began ...   757

Here indeed is the language of real people. Part of it is based on French—the quick interchange of brief utterances is fairly common in French narrative. But the colloquial quality of the language is produced mainly by Chaucer's use of the syntax and style of the English romances.

This is not just a matter of fortmilitic intensifiers ("ryght blythely"), riming tags ("as I kan"), and asseverations ("so God me save"), of which *The Book of the Duchess* has its full measure, even more, as I said, than in *The Romaunt of the Rose*. The reason this dialogue is so lifelike is because of a feature of which there is almost no trace in the *Romaunt*—the fact that it is punctuated with casual blasphemies—such as "by God's half" (that is, "I swear by the wounds in God's side"). This is the sort of thing that shocked Chaucer's Parson—a very similar curse leads him to exclaim, "What eyleth the man, so synfully to swere" (II.1171); but that is the way the heroes of English romance sometimes talked—"For God," says Bevis, "that I nelle." And that is the way real people, perhaps especially aristocrats, talked. English noblemen (even noble churchmen) were notorious for such swearing—the favorite oath of Samson, the famous abbot of Bury St. Edmunds, was "By God's face" (per faciem Dei)—perhaps in an attempt to outdo the king, Henry II, who was most fond of "By God's eyes" (per oculos Dei).[36] Henry II swore in French; Edward III swore in English, or at least he did in that riming motto I mentioned previously:

> Hey, hey the whyte swan!
> By Godes soul I am thy man!

I am not sure about the theology of God's soul, but that fine point evidently did not bother King Edward—nor did it bother Chaucer's Miller nor the clerk Alan in the *Reeve's Tale*, both of whom use exactly the same curse.[37]

There is a great deal of this aristocratic swearing in *The Book of the Duchess*, not just in dialogue but in the voice of the narrator. It is a part of what might be called the expletive style; it involves a heavy use of adverbs ("truly," "indeed," and such), a lot of interjections (I find at least 50 interjections—that is, words grammatically classified as such), and a heavy use of asseverations and expletives. The Lord's name is taken in vain at least 18 times in *The Book of the Duchess*, along with six expletive uses of "Lord," and 14 other oaths—"by my troth," "by the rood," "by the mass," "by Saint John," "by [God's] halwes twelve." That is a lot of cursing.

This is part of the expletive style that Chaucer learned from the popular romances. However, in the romances its most obvious manifestation—the cursing—is usually restricted to the direct representation of the speech of the characters, and the narrators curse but rarely—an occasional harmless "ywis" or "God woot." In *Sir Thopas*, when Chaucer is mocking the style of these romances—playing up its eccentricities—his narrator is quite restrained. He is more fond of fillers ("As it was Goddes grace") and sincere invocation ("God shilde his cors from shonde") than of expletives of any sort. He uses "Loo" once, and the closest he comes to a mild oath is "par charitee."[38] He would not shock the Prioress, whose greatest oath was "by Saint Loy." But he might have been regarded as somewhat prissy by Criseyde, who swears almost as often and enthusiastically as her uncle Pandarus.[39]

She would have approved of the narrator in *The Book of the Duchess*, with his heavily expletive style, including frequently taking the Lord's name in vain. There is almost none of this in the work of Chaucer's contemporaries—Gower never uses the word "God" in an oath in all the 33,444 lines of the *Confessio Amantis*—and almost none outside dialogue even in the English romances. Chaucer's model for this aspect of the narrative voice was not the narrative but the representation of direct speech in the romances—Bevis' "by God that nele I do." Chaucer's narrator is a character in his own right, and his style is based on the vigorous colloquial speech of the characters in English romance rather than that of the narrators.

In short, before Chaucer could learn to make his narrator speak like a gentleman he had to learn how to cuss. And he learned to do so by around 1370 when he wrote *The Book of the Duchess*. The dreamer's and Man in Black's first dialogue is punctuated with casual blasphemy. So is their last one:

> "... Thow wost ful lytel what thou menest;   1305
> I have lost more than thow wenest.
> God wot, allas! Ryght that was she!"

> "Allas, sir, how? What may that be?"
> "She ys ded!" "Nay!" "Yis, be my trouthe!"
> "Is that youre los? Be God, hyt ys routhe!"

> And with that word ryght anoon
> They gan to strake forth; al was doon....

Chaucer's Parson would not have approved, but this is clearly what Wordsworth defined as an adequate poetic style, a "language such as men do use," or at least such as men, and women too, did use in the fourteenth century. *The House of Fame* has even more of this than *The Book of the Duchess*. One gets the impression that Chaucer cussed a blue streak throughout the 1370's. Thereafter, he learned to modulate his cussing, to use it as a means of characterization. But I won't talk about that. That would take me beyond the year 1370, into a time when there is a lot of documentation and a good many texts—the sort of things that tend to get in the way of one's theories. I prefer the earlier decades.[40]

NOTES

1. Derek Pearsall, intro., *The Auchinleck Manuscript: National Library of Scotland Advocates' 19.2.1.* (London: Scholar Press, 1977), p. viii.

2. See Laura Hibbard Loomis, "Chaucer and the Auchinleck Manuscript: Guy of Warwick," in *Essays and Studies in Honor of Carleton Brown* (New York: New York UP, 1940), pp. 111–28.

3. Elizabeth Kirk, "Chaucer and his English Contemporaries," in George D. Economou, ed., *Geoffrey Chaucer: A Collection of Original Articles* (New York: McGraw-Hill, 1975), pp. 111–27.

4. Juliet Vale, *Edward III and Chivalry* (Woodbridge, Suffolk, Eng: Boydell Press, 1982).

5. James I. Wimsatt, ed., *Chaucer and the Poems of "Ch" in Univ. of Pennsylvania US French 15.* (Cambridge: Brewer, 1982).

6. See James I. Wimsatt, *Chaucer and the French Love Poets* (Chapel Hill: U of North Carolina P, 1968).

7. See Larry D. Benson. gen. ed., *The Riverside Chaucer*, 3rd ed. (Boston: Houghton Mifflin, 1987), p. 1081. All quotations from Chaucer are from this edition, as are the abbreviations of the titles of Chaucer's works (see ibid., p. 779).

8. R. H. Robbins, "Geffroi Chaucier, Poete français, Father of English Poetry," *Chaucer Review*, 13 (1978), 93–115.

9. Wimsatt, *Chaucer and the Poems of "Ch*," p. 2.

10. On "aesthetic funding," see S. C. Pepper, *The Basis of Criticism in the Arts* (Cambridge: Harvard UP, 1945), though I have modified his ideas for my own uses.

11. See *The Nun's Priest's Tale*, VII.2879.

12. Rossell H. Robbins, *Secular Lyrics of the Fourteenth and Fifteenth Centuries*, 2nd ed. (Oxford: Clarendon Press, 1955), p. 152.

13. Ezra Pound, *ABC of Reading* (Norfolk, Conn.: New Directions, 1955), p. 106.

14. See the comments on Chaucer's lyrics in *ABC of Reading*, pp. 109–11.

15. Eustache Deschamps, "L'art de dictier," in *Oeuvres completes*, ed. Auguste H. E. Queux de Saint-Hilaire and Gaston Raynaud, *Société des Anciens Textes Française* (Paris: Firmin Didot, 1878–1903), Vol. VII, p. 270.

16. Gervase Mathew, *The Court of Richard II* (London: Murray, 1968), p. 28 (on Richard II's handkerchief). The plural of respectful address is found as early as the thirteenth century, but it begins to become common only in the late fourteenth century.

17. See *Riverside Chaucer, Romaunt of the Rose*, Fragment B, vv. 1883–1992.

18. Cf. *heterli* adv. in *Middle English Dictionary*, ed. Hans Kurath, Sherman Kuhn, John Reidy, and (currently) Robert E. Lewis (Ann Arbor: U of Michigan P, 1954–). The word does appear outside alliterative poetry, but only very rarely in the fourteenth century.

19. However, see Vale, *Edward III and Chivalry* (as in n. 4, above) on the possible relation of *Winner and Waster* with the royal court.

20. *Facsimile of British Museum MS. Harley 2253*, intro. N. R. Ker, Early English Text Society, O.S. 255 (London: Oxford UP, 1965). I have normalized the spelling and made a few changes in capitalization and punctuation.

21. See Derek Brewer, "The Middle English Ideal of Personal Beauty," *Modern Language Quarterly*, 50 (1955), 267–68.

22. *The Harley Lyrics*, ed. G. L. Brook, 3rd edition (Manchester: U of Manchester P, 1964), p. 33.

23. E. T. Donaldson, "The Idiom of Popular Poetry in The Miller's Tale," in *Speaking of Chaucer* (London: Athlone Press, 1970), pp. 13–29.

24. *The Harley Lyrics* (as in note 22, above), pp. 62–63.

25. *The Romance of Sir Bettis of Hamptoun*, ed, Eugen Kölbing, Early English Text Society (London: K. Paul, Trench, Trubner and Co., 1885, 1886, 1894), extra series, 46, 48, 65.

26. *Kyng Alisaundre*, ed. G. V. Smithers, Early English Text Society O.S. 227 and 237 (London: Oxford UP, 1952–1957).

27. See Henry Bradley, "Changes in the Language to the Days of Chaucer," in *Cambridge History of English Literature*, ed. A. W. Ward,

A. R. Waller (Cambridge: Cambridge UP, 1907–27), Vol. 1, pp, 379–406; 399.

28. The dates are those used in *The Middle English Dictionary* (as in note 18, above).

29. Gower's verse has very few touches of the older English style; there are some, of course, since no one writing in the language could entirely escape using them. But Gower seldom uses the formulaic fillers of the English tradition: "never a del," for example, never appears in his work; "ful" and "right" as intensifiers are rare, and "iwis," which Chaucer uses 44 times in his octosyllabics—about 5000 lines—is used only 9 times in all of Gower's *Confessio Amantis*, which is over 33,000 lines. He rarely uses the formulae of the English romances, even such common formulaic similes as "white as milk," "red as rose," "black as jet." Gower uses that pattern only once—"black as sable"—in the whole *Confessio*, whereas Chaucer uses it seven times in the *Romaunt* alone. There are likewise more uses of the formulaic pattern "fair and" (with another adjective) in the *Romaunt* (7) than in the whole *Confessio*. Chaucer's favorite use of that formula is "fair and bright," and, following the English tradition that goes back to Rymenhild the bright in *King Horn* and beyond that to the formulaic use of "beorht" in Anglo-Saxon verse, "bright" is one of Chaucer's favorite epithets for a beautiful lady. Gower uses "bright" only rarely (8 times) and only for "day" or "sun," never for a lady.

30. Derek Brewer, "The Relation of Chaucer to the English and European Traditions," in *Chaucer and Chaucerians*, ed. D. S. Brewer (London: Thomas Nelson, 1966), pp. 2–8.

31. Joseph P. Mersand, *Chaucer's Romance Vocabulary*, 2nd ed. (New York: Comet Press, 1919), p. 91.

32. Derek Brewer, *Chaucer and Chaucerians*, p. 3.

33. *Romaunt*, Fragment B, vv. 2033–42.

34. Cf. *Romaunt*, Fragment B, vv. 2164, 2862, 2844, etc. (for "plesaunce"), 4382, 5807 (for "servage"), 1998, 2044, etc. (for "homage").

35. *RomB*, 1992.

36. Jocelin of Brakelond, *Chronicle*, Camden Soc., 1903, pp. 35, 169, etc.

37. *MilT* I.3132, *RvT* I.4187.

38. In Thopas' own speech, expletives are slightly more common, but not much stronger: "O seinte Marie benedicite" (784), "also moote I thee" (816), "par ma fay" (820).

39. See the chapters on cursing in R. W. V. Elliot, *Chaucer's English* (New York: Academic Press, 1974).

40. In writing this paper, I profited from helpful discussions with Professor Lawrence Besserman and Dr. Jon Whitman of the Hebrew University, and Professor Jerome Mandel of Tel Aviv University. I also owe thanks to Dr. Jacqueline Brown of Cambridge, who saved me from a number of errors.

JOHN H. FISHER

A Language Policy
for Lancastrian England

How did English become the national language of England? From the
Norman Conquest until after 1400, French was the official language of
England—not because any law had been passed to make it so but because
it was the native language of all those who held office. As Sir John
Fortescue explained in 1460, in *De Laudibus Legum Anglie* (I give the
English translation by Stanley Chrimes of Fortescue's Latin):

> [A]fter the French had, by duke William the Conqueror,
> obtained the land, they would not permit advocates to plead
> their causes unless in the language they themselves knew,
> which all advocates do in France, even in the court and
> parliament there. Similarly, after their arrival in England, the
> French did not accept accounts of their revenues, unless in
> their own idiom, lest they should be deceived thereby. They
> took no pleasure in hunting, nor in other recreations, such as
> games of dice or ball, unless carried on in their own
> language. So the English contracted the same habit from
> frequenting such company, so that they to this day speak the
> French language in such games and accounting. (115)

From 1066 until 1217, England was the property of the dukes of Normandy, who were in turn subjects of the kings of France. The French connection was so strong that when Pope Innocent III divested Duke Jean, whom we call King John, of his lordship, he ordered the French king to carry out the sentence; and when the barons fell out with John over the implementation of the Magna Cliarta, they offered the English crown to King Louis of France, who came over to England to take possession. England ceased to be a province of France when William Marshall defeated King Louis in the Battle of Lincoln in 1217.

We think of the period from 1066 to 1350 as culturally barren in England, but some of the most important literature of that period was produced for the Anglo-Norman aristocracy that flourished on both sides of the Channel. *Chanson de Roland*, Arthurian romances, troubadour lyrics, the first French play, French sermons, saints' lives, and chronicles are found in insular manuscripts and were probably written in England, and some of the fittest French writers—Chrétien de Troyes, Marie de France, Robert Grosseteste, and in Chaucer's time Jean Froissart, John Mandeville, and John Gower—wrote French in England for Anglo-Norman audiences (Merilees; Legge).

The fourteenth century saw the beginning of the rebirth of English cultural independence, but the reigns of Edward III and Richard II, 1327–99, were the high point of the influence of French culture in England (Johnson; Vale; Matthew). As Ruskin observes in *The Stones of Venice*, it is when a culture is decaying that it articulates itself most clearly. After King John lost Normandy, he and his successors still claimed lordship over France south of the Loire, for which they were obliged to do homage to the French king. And beginning with Edward III, for a hundred years the English kings asserted, and tried to implement, their sovereignty over France.

This was the great era of French influence throughout Europe. The geographical centrality of France, the wealth and population its fertile lands generated in an agricultural economy, its supremacy in chivalry, when a knight in armor was equivalent to a modern tank, made France the superpower of the Continent. But a superpower in the medieval tribal sense. Until long after Chaucer's death there was no unified "France," only a kaleidoscope of competing dukedoms, of which the English were merely the most disruptive. French nationalism is not considered to have begun to emerge until Joan of Arc (c. 1430), whereas English nationalism began to emerge in the 1340s, with Edward III.

Even though most of the energy of France during this period of cultural ascendancy was spent on internal conflict, enough was left to spill over onto its neighbors. When the pope and his curia moved to Avignon in 1309, France became the seat of religious as well as secular supremacy. Its modes of combat, architecture, religion, literature, dress, food, and manners set the standard everywhere, and especially in England, which had for so long been an integral part of France.

Men of the English aristocracy regularly married Continental wives and married their own daughters off to Continental husbands. King Edward's wife, Philippa, came from Hainault in modern Belgium. Froissart served as her secretary from 1361 until her death in 1369 and while in England began collecting material for his chronicle of the Hundred Years' War. Chaucer's wife, Philippa, and her sister Katherine were the daughters of a French knight, Sir Paon de Roet, who came to England in the retinue of Queen Philippa. One wonders what the domestic language was in Sir Paon's household, in which Philippa grew up, and what Chaucer's own domestic language may have been when he married the daughter of a French knight. Katherine married Sir Thomas Swynford and became the mistress, and eventually the wife, of John of Gaunt and mother of Henry Beaufort and his brothers, who, I argue, played an important part in the reestablishment of English.

Below this international aristocratic stratum, the English commonality were beginning to assert their own culture. It was English-speaking longbowmen who had cut down the French chivalry at Crécy and Poitiers. An argument used in the English parliaments of 1295, 1344, 1346, and 1376 for support in the wars against France was that French victory would annihilate the English language (Fisher, "Chancery and the Emergence" 879). The Rolls of Parliament were regularly in Latin and French, but occasional entries indicate that the discussion was in English. In an entry of 1426, the exposition is in Latin, but the lines spoken by the witnesses are in English. In another of 1432, the clerks of the Royal Chapel present a petition in Latin, but the introduction is in English. In 1362 the clerks admitted for the first time that Parliament was addressed in English, and in the same year Parliament decreed that all legal proceedings had to be carried on in English because the litigants could not understand French. As a matter of fact, this statute was not enforced, and the common-law courts continued to plead in French until 1731, but that is another story.[1]

Evidently by the 1360s most oral exchange in commerce and government must have been carried on in English, but the records were still kept in Latin and French. Formal education was in Latin, and the writing masters who taught English clerks the secretarial skills of *ars dictaminis* taught them in Latin and French. Virtually all religious and cultural writings intended for any kind of circulation were in Latin or French. Such records as we have of the libraries of Edward III and Richard II and other books mentioned in wills and inventories before 1400 are exclusively Latin and French. A. S. G. Edwards and Derek Pearsall estimate that there are extant only some thirty manuscripts of secular poetry in English written before 1400 and that nearly all are personal productions, like Cotton Nero A.X of the *Gawain* poems, King's College 13 of *William of Palerne*, and Bodley 264 of the *Alexander*. A. I. Doyle has pointed out that the few extant manuscripts of secular poetry in English before 1400 are by household scribes writing in provincial dialects, not by professional scribes in London. The courtesy literature that distinguished the gentle from the churl was virtually all in French (Nicholls).

It is the politics of the movement of the written language from Latin and French to English that concerns me here. We are not now talking about when secular poetry began to be composed in English. From 1300 on, and particularly after 1350, more and more literature was composed in English, but clearly there was no audience that caused these English writings to be copied and disseminated. All the manuscripts of Geoffrey Chaucer, John Mandeville, John Trevisa, John Barbour, Laurence Minot, and other fourteenth-century secular English authors date from after 1400. Gower might be regarded as an exception because one of the two earliest manuscripts of *Confessio Amantis* (the Stafford manuscript, now Huntington El 26.A.17) seems to be dedicated to Henry Bolingbroke before he became king in 1399, but that is grist to my mill.

A great deal has been written about the emergence of writing in English after 1350, perhaps best in *A History of the English Language* by Albert Baugh, now revised and updated by Thomas Cable, but like all others, Baugh and Cable write as if English just happened. They trace a gradual accretion of statements about English and documents in English that reveal an undirected, populist movement. The model of Chaucer used to be given a large role in this transition, and Derek Pearsall gives Lydgate almost as much importance in conferring prestige on literary

English. But neither Baugh and Cable nor Pearsall, nor any others who have discussed the matter, point to the significance of the relation between the specific date at which manuscripts of English writings began to multiply and the date of the Lancastrian usurpation of the throne, in September 1399. Until 1400 we have virtually no manuscripts of poetry in English that were commercially prepared and intended for circulation. Immediately after 1400 we have the manuscripts of Gower, Chaucer, and other fourteenth-century writers and the compositions and manuscripts of Lydgate; Hoccleve; Clanvowe; Scogan; John Walton; Edward, Duke of York; and other fifteenth-century writers. After 1420 the libraries of Sir Richard Beauchamp, Sir Thomas Chaworth, Sir Edmund Rede, and Sir John Paston contained manuscripts by Chaucer and Lydgate as well as other courtly and didactic writings in English (Doyle).

I do not believe that this sudden burst of production in English after 1400 was simply a natural evolution. I think that it was encouraged by Henry IV, and even more by Henry V, as a deliberate policy intended to engage the support of Parliament and the English citizenry for a questionable usurpation of the throne. The publication of Chaucer's poems and his enshrinement as the perfecter of rhetoric in English were central to this effort. The evidence is circumstantial. King Henry, Prince Henry, Henry Beaufort, John Lydgate, Thomas Chaucer, and Thomas Hoccleve did not keep diaries about their plans and motives, but the associations and dates warrant examination.

The fragility of the reign of Henry IV is well known (Wylie, vol. 1; Harriss, *Cardinal*, ch. 2). During the first four years he had to contend with three rebellions of barons who rejected his title to the throne. He countered these by appealing to the commons for support, thus ultimately strengthening parliamentary government. One aspect of this appeal was increased use of the English vernacular. The earliest English entry in the Rolls of Parliament is the 1388 petition of the Mercers Guild printed by Chambers and Daunt, but the next English entries are the 1397 address of Judge Rickbill concerning the impeachment of the duke of Gloucester, which precipitated the downfall of Richard II; two 1399 addresses by Chief Justice Thirnyng regarding the deposition of Richard; and—most important of all—Henry's own challenge to the throne on 30 September 1399 (Fisher, "Chancery and the Emergence" 880). The only conceivable reason for these entries to be recorded in

English at a time when the official entries in the Rolls were still uniformly in Latin and French was to appeal to the commons.

John Gower says that Richard II encouraged him to write the *Confessio Amantis* in English (Fisher, *Gower* 9–11), but the earliest manuscript (Huntington El.26, mentioned above) appears to have been presented to Henry Bolingbroke upon his return from France in 1399. It is illuminated with the lion recognizance of John of Gaunt and the swan of Thomas of Gloucester, which Bolingbroke assumed immediately after the murder of Gloucester. The absence of royal emblems indicates that the manuscript was completed before Henry's coronation. Immediately after the coronation, Gower composed *In Praise of Peace*, a poem in English warning Henry not to presume on the right of conquest but to seek peace and to rule with pity (Fisher, *Gower* 132–33). Between the time of Henry's accession and Gower's death in 1408, Gower commissioned perhaps ten manuscripts of his *Confessio* and other English poems. Richard Firth Green in *Poets and Princepleasers* has a good deal to say about Gower's support of Henry's usurpation.

In 1393 Henry had given Gower a collar with a swan pendant, apparently as a reward for Gower's support of Thomas of Gloucester, and soon after his coronation he granted Gower two pipes of wine yearly (21 Nov. 1399). At nearly the same time (13 Oct. 1399[2]) the King doubled Chaucer's annuity from Richard to £20 and granted to Hoccleve, then a young clerk in privy seal, an annuity of £10 (12 Nov. 1399). Henry IV may have made these grants for the writers' civil service rather than for their poetry, but his benefactions to Gower, Chaucer, and Hoccleve all three certainly qualify him as a supporter of English-poets.

Our attention now shifts to Henry V who came to the throne in 1413. The entries in the Rolls of Parliament under Henry IV continued to be mostly in French, and Henry V continued to use French for his correspondence as Prince of Wales and during the first three years of his reign. His effort to secure the support of the commons in Parliament was even more strenuous than that of his father: in 1414 he granted that their statutes should be made without altering the language of the petitions on which the statutes were based. There is no recorded evidence that this elevated the use of English, but petitions and the actions upon them are the primary constituents of the Rolls of Parliament, whose earliest entry in English is the mercers' petition of 1388, as mentioned above. Henry V's success at Agincourt in 1415, after so many years of failure in the wars with France, reinforced English nationalism, and in 1416, as the king began to assemble his forces to make good his claim to the French throne, he addressed five proclamations in English to the citizens of London, requesting supplies and commanding soldiers and sailors to assemble for the invasion.[3] These are the first royal proclamations in English since the proclamation of Henry III in 1258 and that had been the only one since the last English proclamation of William the Conqueror in 1087. Most significant, upon reaching France on 12 August 1417, Henry addressed his first missive in English to his chancellor, and from that time until his death in 1422 he used English in nearly all his correspondence with the government and the citizens of London and other English cities. The use of English by Henry V marks the turning point in establishing English as the national language of England. Its effect is reflected in the familiar entry of 1422 in the abstract book of the Brewers Guild explaining their change of record keeping from Latin to English:

> Whereas our mother-tongue, to wit the English tongue, hath in modern days begun to be honorably enlarged and adorned, for that our most excellent lord, King Henry V, hath in his letters missive and divers affairs touching his own person, more willingly chosen to declare the secrets of his will, for the better understanding of his people, hath with a diligent mind procured the common idiom (setting aside others) to be commended by the exercise of writing; and there are many of our craft of Brewers who have the knowledge of writing and reading in the said English idiom, but in others, to wit, the Latin and French, before these times used, they do not in any wise understand. For which causes with many others, it being considered how that the greater part of the Lords and trusty Commons have begun to make their matters to be noted down in our mother tongue, so we also in our craft, following in some manner their steps, have decreed to commit to memory the needful things which concern us [in English].
>
> (Chambers and Daunt 139)

This momentous decision is recorded in Latin, but in the 1420s the Brewers and other guilds did switch their record keeping to English, and the chancery dialect, modeled in many ways on Henry's own idiom and spelling (Richardson; Fisher, Richardson, and Fisher), became the prestige written language (Samuels). Chambers and Daunt edited many of these documents in their *Book of London English*, and John Fisher, Malcolm Richardson, and Jane Fisher edited Henry's signet letters and other English chancery documents in their *Anthology of Chancery English*.

This is the documented historical record, but I believe that the transformation of the language of government and business would not have been possible without more than a decade of preparation and propaganda. Let us go back to 1398, when Prince Henry was eleven years old. According to a tradition commencing with the Chronicle of John Rous, completed in 1477, Henry Beaufort (son of John of Gaunt and Katherine Swynford and therefore half brother to Henry IV, son of John of Gaunt and Blanche of Lancaster) was tutor to Prince Henry at Queen's College, Oxford. The relationships with Beaufort and the university are not mentioned in any other chronicle, and Rous's account—coming, as it does, some eighty years after the event—is rightly regarded as questionable evidence. It may be pointed out, however, that since Rous was born in 1411 and at Oxford by 1425, his testimony is more current than the 1477 date of his chronicle might indicate. Nineteenth-century biographers accepted both relationships (e.g., Armitage-Smith 414; Towle 170–71); recent biographers accept the tutorship but not the prince's residence at Oxford (e.g., Harriss, *Cardinal* 9; Hutchinson 18; Seward 4). The careful conclusion of the entry on Beaufort in the *Dictionary of National Biography* suggests why Harriss and others have accepted the tutorship:

> [Beaufort] is said to have been the tutor of the Prince of Wales. He certainly exercised considerable influence over him. While the king was in a great measure guided by Arundel, the prince attached himself to the younger and more popular party of which [Beaufort] was the head.

In the entry on Henry V, the *DNB* narrows the inference:

> The tradition that he was educated at Queen's College, Oxford, under the care of his uncle Henry Beaufort ... first appears in the "Chronicle of John Rous" (ed. Hearne, p. 207). Beaufort was chancellor [of Oxford] in 1398, and, if the statement is correct, the prince's residence at Oxford must

have fallen in this year. There is, however, no record relating to Henry at Queen's College.

Again the evidence is circumstantial. The political association between Henry and Beaufort from 1403 onward, abundantly detailed and documented in Harriss's *Cardinal Beaufort*, was so constant and familiar that biographers feel they must accept a personal relationship, hence the tutorship; but the lack of any record at Oxford makes them shy away from the Queen's College association. One might ask, Why accept one half of Rous's statement but not the other? And would it have been that unusual for the college records not to mention a boy of eleven—even a prince—staying with his uncle and having no official connection with Oxford? Hutchinson (17) and Seward (3) never consider where and when the tutorship that they accept might have occurred. As the *DNB* observes, the best possibility is 1398, when Beaufort was chancellor of Oxford.

In the fall of 1398, at the age of twenty-three, Henry Beaufort was made Bishop of Lincoln and began his service with the king. But Harriss surmises that Beaufort still spent a good deal of time in Oxford until 1403, when he was appointed chancellor of England for the first time (*Cardinal* 8, 12, 19). He served as chancellor four times—under Henry IV, V, and VI—becoming the richest man in England and supplying enormous sums to support the war in France. Until his death in 1447, according to the historian William Stubbs, "he held the strings of English policy" (3: 143). K. B. McFarlane's essay "At the Deathbed of Cardinal Beaufort" is a fascinating overview of Beaufort's wealth and influence (115–38).

Prince Henry was not at Oxford continuously after 1398. In October of that year King Richard, after banishing Henry Bolingbroke and confiscating the Lancastrian holdings, called the prince to court and in January 1399 took young Henry with him on his expedition to Ireland. There Henry remained until his victorious father sent a ship for him the next October. After Henry had been created Prince of Wales on 15 October 1399, he is reported at Chester and in Wales with the troops from time to time, but until 1403 his connection with the Welsh wars was nominal. The actual operations were in the imperious hands of Sir Henry Percy (Hotspur). It was the rebellion of the Percys that led to Prince Henry's appointment in March 1403 as King's Lieutenant of the Marches of Wales, making him at sixteen commander in chief in fact as

well as in name (Harriss, *Cardinal* 15; Seward 18). We have no
continuous account of Prince Henry's whereabouts between October
1399 and March 1403. In the same month that the prince assumed
military command, Henry Beaufort was named chancellor of England
for the first time. So whatever period there could have been for Henry
Beaufort and Prince Henry to contemplate the place of English in
Lancastrian policy would have been in whatever intervals they may have
passed together at Queen's College and elsewhere between 1398 and
1403.

During this five years Thomas Chaucer was settling into his manor
at Ewelme, about ten miles from Oxford.[4] Thomas was the son of
Philippa Chaucer, the sister of Katherine Swynford. We will not here go
into the question of whether his father was Geoffrey Chaucer or John of
Gaunt, but Thomas was at least first cousin to the Beauforts and may
have been an unacknowledged half brother of both, the Beauforts and
the king (Fisher, *Importance* 19–23). His amazing career points in this
direction. In 1395 he was married to a wealthy heiress, Maud Bergersh,
through whom he acquired Ewelme and many other valuable properties,
and he was showered with honors from the moment Henry IV assumed
the throne: in 1399 he was appointed Constable of Wallingford Castle,
in 1400 Sheriff of Oxfordshire, in 1402 King's Butler, with responsibility
not only for procuring and dispensing the wine for the royal household
but also for collecting petty customs, the tax on wine imports throughout the kingdom. He sat as member of Parliament for Oxfordshire in
1401 and in thirteen other parliaments. He was Speaker for the
Commons in the Parliament of 1407 and in three other parliaments and
remained, until his death in 1434, an important intermediary between
the commons and the king.

A third member of Prince Henry's putative Oxford circle between
1398 and 1403 may have been John Lydgate. We know that he was at
Gloucester College, Oxford, in 1406 from a letter by the prince to the
abbot and chapter of Bury Saint Edmunds asking them to allow Lydgate
to continue his studies at Oxford (Pearsall 29), and John Norton-Smith
supposes that Lydgate was in residence there from 1397 to 1408 (195).

Thomas Chaucer was one of Lydgate's longtime patrons, and by all
accounts the two sustained a pleasant relationship at Ewelme (see
Schirmer; Pearsall; and Ebin). Thomas's manor was the salon for a
literate Lancastrian circle much interested in English poetry, from whose
members Lydgate received several commissions. In the complimentary

Balade at the Departyng of Thomas Chaucer into France, he extolled Thomas as his "maister dere," the same term he applied several times to Geoffrey. The "balade" to Thomas Chaucer, like the close relationship between Prince Henry and Henry Beaufort, is circumstantial evidence for an association dating back to college. An Oxford association of the prince, his tutor, his cousin, and the budding poet-apologist for the house of Lancaster could have been the time and place when the seeds for the self-conscious cultivation of English as the national language were planted. And the first sprout of that momentous plan may have been the decision to organize and publish the poetry of Geoffrey Chaucer.

There are no extant manuscripts of Chaucer's poems dating from before his death in 1400, and it is the general (though by no means universal) opinion today that he died without commissioning a presentation copy of a single one of his works (Fisher, "Animadversions"). Why we do not know, since presentation of an elaborate manuscript to a patron was the accepted method of publication in the Middle Ages (Root). Chaucer's failure to publish, or the loss of all his presentation manuscripts, is one of the great mysteries of early English literary culture. Furthermore, the textual evidence seems to indicate that Chaucer fully finished very few of his works, either poetry or prose (Fisher, "Animadversions"; Blake; Windeatt). He was living in Westminster during the first two years of the fateful 1398–1403 period, presumably surrounded by copies of works that were well known to the courtly and commercial circles of London from oral presentations dating back over thirty years but that had never been published because of his own diffidence and because of the lack of prestige of English as a cultivated language. Everyone spoke English, but writing in English was simply not couth.

This is not an unusual sociolinguistic situation. It was exhibited in Montreal and India and Norway at the beginning of this century.[5] In Montreal most of the population spoke French, but business and commercial writing was largely in English. In Norway most of the population spoke Norwegian dialects but wrote Danish. In India most of the population spoke Prakrit dialects, of which Hindi was the most widespread, but official writing was in English. In these cultures in the nineteenth century and for some time afterward, the populace generally spoke native dialects, but official and polite writing was in nonnative prestige languages. So it was with England until after 1400.

French, Norwegian, and Hindi are now official languages in these cultures and are exemplified by increasingly sophisticated literatures. But the elevation of these languages is not the result merely of demographic and economic evolution. It reflects deliberate political decisions. We have ample evidence about these decisions today, but the absence of evidence for the England of 1400 does not mean that the process was different at that time. England had persisted in its bilingual situation, with French as the official language and English as a patois, for four hundred years, two hundred after the Battle of Lincoln made the country politically independent and sixty after the beginning of the Hundred Years' War made France its enemy. It seems likely that bilingualism might have persisted for much longer if it had not been for a deliberate decision by some influential authority.

Henry V was such an authority. Much has been made of his charisma as a national hero, of his cultivation of nationalism, of his communication with Parliament and the citizenry (Harriss, *Henry V*). It took him three years after his accession to implement the use of English in his signet letters. This action can hardly have been casual and unpremeditated. There is a persistent medieval tradition that official languages were inaugurated by kings—by King Alfred in Anglo-Saxon England (Richards), by Philip the Fair in France (Brunot 1: 370), by Alphonse X in Spain (Wolff 178; Fisher, "European Chancelleries"). Modern linguists tend to discount this tradition and to attribute sociolinguistic developments to impersonal demographic and economic forces. I do not deny the importance of such forces, but I think that (whatever the process in Montreal) the development of Norwegian would not have proceeded as it did without the leadership of Knud Knudsen and Ivar Asen, nor of Hindi without the leadership of B. J. Tilak and Mahatma Gandi (see n5). Einar Haugen discusses specifically the role of the language planner and cites the names of language planners in northern European countries and in Greece and Turkey (168–70). The history of the developments of all official languages for which there is documentation show that such developments do not occur without influential leadership and deliberate political process,

The outburst of copying and composing in English that began soon after 1400 can best be explained as a deliberately instigated activity that laid the groundwork for the political actions of 1416–22. That Chaucer should be chosen as the cynosure for this movement would not be at all surprising. He was of both the royal and the commercial circles, son of a vintner and a close relative by marriage to King Henry IV, Prince Henry, and the Beauforts. His vernacular poetry had already attracted attention by Thomas Usk, Henry Scogan, John Clanvowe, and other contemporaries in England and by Eustach Deschamps in France. Norman Blake, developing the arguments of J. S. P. Tatlock, Germaine Dempster, A. I. Doyle, Malcolm Parkes, and others, has given a persuasive account of the evolution of the text of the *Canterbury Tales* from the initial effort to make sense of the foul papers in the Hengwrt manuscript to the fully edited text in the Ellesmere manuscript. He envisages this process of development through five or six versions as progressing under the direction of a group of editors working to give a veneer of completeness to papers that Chaucer had left in disarray at the time of his death.

The most sumptuous of all Chaucer manuscripts, Ellesmere, written by the same scribe as Hengwrt, is associated by its illuminations and scrimshaw with Thomas Chaucer, whom Manly and Rickert propose as "logically the person to have made what was clearly intended as an authoritative text" (1: 159). Thomas would presumably have had opportunities to visit with his father during the poet's last years in Westminster and to arrange for the Hengwrt scribe to begin making an initial compilation from the foul papers. He and his friends (Henry Beaufort, Prince Henry?) could have gone over the result with the scribe and engaged another scribe to produce the Corpus version; then gone through a similar process with that and with the Harlean, Lansdowne, and two Cambridge versions—I am using Blake's scenario. With the last two they approached completion: Cambridge Dd achieved the Ellesmere order for the tales, and Cambridge Gg introduced the first illustrations of the pilgrims. Having got to this stage, Thomas Chaucer could have arranged for the original scribe to produce the Ellesmere manuscript, incorporating all the editorial "improvements" arrived at throughout the several versions.

This process would have been expensive, but Thomas Chaucer had the money to pay for it. Doyle and Parkes give a fascinating account of a group of five scribes working in London and Westminster in the first quarter of the century who produced eight of the earliest manuscripts of the *Canterbury Tales*, including four of those that Blake treats in his scenario of the evolution of the text (Hg, El, Cp, and Ha). One or more of the same group of scribes also produced a copy of *Troylus and Criseyde*, seven copies of *Confessio Amantis*, a copy of *Piers*

Plowman, a copy of John Trevisa's translation of Bartholomaeus Anglicus, and three manuscripts of the writings of Thomas Hoccleve. Indeed, as one of the group himself, Hoccleve cooperated in producing the Trinity College manuscript of *Confessio Amantis* that Doyle and Parkes use as the touchstone for their analysis.

Doyle and Parkes's evidence indicates that the London book trade at the beginning of the fifteenth century was still very informal. The shifting associations among the scribes militates against the notion of bookshops employing regular staffs of copyists. It appears, instead, that books were produced under individual contract. The contractors were called "stationers" because they were stationary; that is, they had shops where they could be reached. Paul Christianson is assembling evidence of these shops clustered around Saint Paul's Church in London. There the stationers accepted commissions from patrons for books or other documents, which they copied themselves and hired other scribes to help with. The assistants worked on a piecework basis, fascicle by fascicle, in their own rooms. When the copying was complete, the stationer would assemble the fascicles and send them out to the limners to be decorated, and eventually to the binders to be bound. Most of the piecework clerks would be, like Hoccleve, regularly employed in governmental or commercial offices. Some, like Doyle and Parkes's scribe D, might be free-lance scriveners.

This commercial method of book production had begun long before 1400, but until then its products in England had all been in Latin or French. We have no evidence that the switch to English was stimulated by any policy of Henry IV, Prince Henry, or Henry Beaufort. None of the manuscripts by the five scribes identified by Doyle and Parkes reveals any connection with royalty, but royalty and aristocracy were patrons for English manuscripts. The Morgan manuscript of *Troylus and Criseyde* has on its first page the arms of Prince Henry while he was still Prince of Wales. And the English poetry composed at the beginning of the century shows that Prince Henry was considered a patron and Geoffrey Chaucer the initiator. G. L. Harriss observes that Hoccleve's *Regement of Princes* was completed in 1411 and Lydgate's *Troy Book* was commissioned in 1412, precisely the years "in which the prince, at the head of a council of his own choosing and virtually without reference to his father, was carrying through a sustained programme of 'bone governance' to which he had pledged himself in the parliament of January 1410" (*Henry V* 9). Part of the "bone governance" may have been the enhancement of the position of English.

This takes us back to the third member of the putative Oxford circle, John Lydgate. Lydgate's dedication of the *Troy Book* comes as close as anything we have to attributing to Prince Henry a nationalistic policy for enhancing the use of English. The prince, Lydgate says,

> Whyche me comaunded the drery pitus fate
> Of hem of Troye in englysche, to translate
> . . . .
> By-cause he wolde that to hyge and lowe
> The noble story openly wer knowe
> In oure tonge, aboute in every age,
> And y-writen as wel in oure langage
> As in latyn or in frensche it is;
> That of the story the trouthe we nat mys
> No more than doth eche other nacioun:
> This was the fyn of his entencioun.
>   (*Troy Book*, Pro. 105–06, 111–18)

Schirmer identifies the Tanner D.2 manuscript of this poem as the possible presentation copy to Henry himself (50). Lydgate's *Life of Our Lady* is likewise in one manuscript ascribed to the "excitation and stirryng of our worshipful prince, kyng Harry the fifthe." Even though Pearsall doubts the validity of this ascription, because the work was never finished and contains no internal reference to the patron such as Lydgate usually makes (Pearsall 286), the ascription manifests recognition of Henry's patronage of English letters.

What is most significant to my argument, however, is Lydgate's acknowledgment that his version of the Troy story expands on Chaucer's model:

> The hoole story Chaucer kan yow telle
> Yif that ye liste, no man bet alyve,
> Nor the processe halfe so wel discryve,
> For he owre englishe gilte with his sawes,
> Rude and boistous firste be olde dawes,
> That was ful fer from al perfeccioun,
> And but of litel reputaticoun,
> Til that he cam & thorug his poetrie,

Gan oure tonge firste to magnifie,
And adourne it with his elloquence—
To whom honour, laude, & reverence,
Thorug-oute this londe yove be & songe,
So that the laurer of oure englishe tonge
Be to hym yove for his excellence,
Rigt as whilom by fill hige sentence
Perpetuelly for a memorial.
    (*Troy Book* 3.4234–19)

Two of Lydgate's earliest poems, *The Complaint of the Black Knight* and *The Flour of Curtesye*, dated by Schirmer between 1400 and 1402—during the fateful 1398–1403 period—are acts of homage to Chaucer (Schirmer 34, 37). The acknowledgment in *The Flour of Curtesye* suggests that they may have been composed very soon after Chaucer's death:

Ever as I call supprise in myn herte
Alway with feare betwyxt drede and shame
Leste oute of lose, any worde asterte
In this metre, to make it seme lame,
Chaucer is deed that had suche a name
Of fayre makyng that [was] without wene
Fayrest in our tonge, as the Laurer grene.

We may assay forto countrefete
His gay style but it wyl not be;
The welle is drie, with the lycoure swete....
    (Spurgeon 1.15)

In *The Churl and the Bird* (c. 1408), a beast fable somewhat like the *Nun's Priest's Tale*, Lydgate again does obeisance to Chaucer's precedence in creating an English that could stand beside French:

Go gentill quayer, and Recommaunde me
Unto my maistir with humble affectioun
Beseke hym lowly of mercy and pite
Of thy rude makyng to have compassioun
And as touching thy translacioun
Oute of frensh / hough ever the englisshe be

Al thing is saide undir correctioun
With supportacioun of your benignite.
   (Spurgeon 1.15)

Schirmer observes that these poems, like most others by Lydgate, must have been written in response to commissions, but he does not venture who the patrons might have been (31, 37). I would like to think that the poems were commissioned by Henry Beaufort and Prince Henry at the same time that they were encouraging Thomas Chaucer to bring out his father's works.

The *Temple of Glas*, another early work acknowledging Chaucer's inspiration, could likewise have been composed in response to the Oxford inspiration. In addition, Lydgate pays tribute to his master Chaucer in the *Serpent of Division* (c. 1420) and the *Siege of Thebes* (c. 1422), whose patrons are not identified; in the *Pilgrimage of the Life of Man* (c. 1427), written for Thomas Montacute, the husband of Chaucer's granddaughter Alice; and in the *Fall of Princes* (c. 1431), for Humphry, duke of Gloucester, the youngest brother of Henry V. The list of Lydgate's patrons reads like a Who's Who of both the courtly and the commercial circles in England, suggesting influential support from the Lancastrian affinity for the cultivation of English. If this support stemmed from policy established at Oxford about 1400 by Henry Beaufort and Prince Henry—a resolve to elevate the prestige of English and to display Chaucer's poetry as the cynosure of this elevation—then John Lydgate could be considered the public relations agent for this policy.

And Lydgate was not alone in his promotional efforts. I have already mentioned Thomas Hoccleve as one of the scribes in the cohort that was turning out commercial manuscripts in English. Hoccleve's relation to the emergence of English is peculiar. As a clerk in the Westminster office of the privy seal, he should have been party to the introduction of English into chancery. But after he retired from the office, about 1425, he compiled a formulary with examples of different kinds of instruments issued by the privy seal office. These examples are all in French or Latin, but between folios 36 and 37 there is a scrap of vellum in Hoccleve's hand with one of the earliest statements about chancery procedure, showing that chancery was a cultivated style:

In a precedende write word by word and leter by leter titel by titel as the copie is & than look ther be aplid ther on in the chauncerie & that the write be retourned unto the chauncerie and begin thus ...

(Fisher, "Chancery Standard" 141)

The instructions go on, in increasingly illegible script, to address themselves to Latin formulas. Hoccleve's professional languages were always, like Chaucer's, Latin and French, while, like Chaucer, he wrote his poetry in English. Like Lydgate, Hoccleve acknowledged Prince Henry as the patron of English and Chaucer as its initiator. *The Regement of Princes* begins with a warm dedication to "[h]ye and noble prince excellent" (2017) and speaks of the prince's grandfather, John of Gaunt, and father, Henry IV (3347–53), indicating that the poem was completed before 1413, when Prince Henry ascended to the throne. Halfway through the dedication comes the first reference to Chaucer: "Mi dere maistir—god his soule quyte!—/ And fadir, Chaucer, fayn wolde han me taght;/ But I was dul and lerned lite or naght" (2077–79). The dedication ends with more compliments to the prince and good wishes for his reign, leading into what Jerome Mitchell has called "virtually the first full-fledged English manual of instruction for a prince" (31), which was of great interest to the public (more than forty manuscripts are extant) because the behavior of the king was the only context in which people of that period could conceive of social amelioration. The discussion continues to be punctuated with direct exhortations to Prince Henry both to be virtuous and to pay Hoccleve his annuity. Near the end, under the heading "take counsel," comes the most explicit tribute to Chaucer, accompanied by the famous picture that is thought to be the exemplar for the Ellesmere and other contemporary portraits:

> The firste fyndere of our faire langage,
> Hath seyde in caas semblable, & othir moo,
> So hyly wel, that it is my dotage
> ffor to expresse or touche any of thoo.
> Alasse! my fadir fro the worlde is goo—
> Be thou my advoket for hym, hevenes quene!
> (Regement 4978–83)

Hoccleve wrote five other poems addressed to Henry V after the king ascended to the throne.

Much more could be written—indeed, has been written (e.g., Bennett)—about the efflorescence of composition and multiplication of manuscripts in English in the first quarter of the fifteenth century. I have said nothing about Henry Scogan's *Moral Balade*, addressed to Prince Henry and his brothers, which also acknowledges "my maister Chaucer." But my line of argument is by this time evident. Hoccleve, no more than Lydgate, [n]ever articulated for the Lancastrian rulers a policy of encouraging the development of English as a national language or of citing Chaucer as the exemplar for such a policy. But we have the documentary and literary evidence of what happened. The linkage of praise for Prince Henry as a model ruler concerned about the use of English and of master Chaucer as the "firste fyndere of our faire langage"; the sudden appearance of manuscripts of the *Canterbury Tales*, *Troylus and Criseyde*, and other English writings composed earlier but never before published; the conversion to English of the signet clerks of Henry V, the chancery clerks, and eventually the guild clerks; and the burgeoning of composition in English and the patronage of that literature by the Lancastrian court circle—these are concurrent historical events. The only question is whether the concurrence was coincidental or deliberate.

All linguistic changes of this sort for which we have documentation—in Norway, India, Canada, Finland, Israel, or elsewhere—have been the result of deliberate, official policy. There is no reason to suppose that the situation was different in England. Policy in the Middle Ages originated with the king, who worked with the advice of influential counselors (Scanlon). As we look at England between 1399 and 1422, we see Henry IV and Henry V attempting to establish their shaky administration by appealing to Parliament, the Beaufort brothers and Thomas Chaucer providing counsel and support, the poetry of Thomas's father being cited as the cynosure of cultivated English, and Henry V beginning to use English for his official missives. An association of Prince Henry, Henry Beaufort, Thomas Chaucer, and John Lydgate at Oxford and Ewelme between 1398 and 1403 would have offered an appropriate opportunity for the initiation of a plan to cultivate English as the official and prestige language of the nation. Oh to have been a cricket on the hearth at Queen's College and Ewelme Manor to have heard the talk that went round the fire in those years![6]

NOTES

1. Pollock and Maitland summarize the history of English legal language (1:80–87). Fisher gives citations for the English records in the Rolls of Parliament and statistics on the increasing number of English entries in the Rolls, from one in 1403 to fifteen in 1449 ("Chancery and the Emergence" 880).

2. The date on the vellum is 13 Oct. 1399, but Ferris shows that the grant was made in Feb. 1400 and backdated to Oct. 1399.

3. The 1416 proclamations and later English missives from Henry V in the London Corporation's Letter Books are printed by Riley.

4. On Thomas Chaucer, see Ruud; Baugh; Roskell; Crow and Olson 541–44. The *DNB* gives a substantial listing of Thomas's many grants and offices, as do Wylie and Waugh, app. E, and McFarlane 96–101. On the close association between Thomas Chaucer and Henry Beaufort, see Harriss, *Cardinal* 20 and index.

5. Heller discusses the development of French as the official language in Montreal; Haugen the development of Norwegian Riksmal (ch. 6); and Misra the spread of Hindi. Grillo treats peripheral and prestige languages in Great Britain and France. Wardhaugh treats not only the rise to dominance of English in Great Britain and French in France but the competition of languages for dominance in Belgium, Switzerland, Canada, and African countries. Cooper devotes a whole volume to the politics of language change.

6. This essay began as a convocation address at Indiana State University, Terre Haute, in April 1991. It develops material presented in *The Importance of Chaucer*.

WORKS CITED

Armitage-Smith, Sidney. *John of Gaunt*. 1904. New York: Barnes, 1964.

Baugh, Albert C. "Kirk's Life Records of Chaucer." *PMLA* 47 (1932): 461–515.

Baugh, Albert C., and Thomas Cable. *A History of The English Language*. 3rd ed. New York: Prentice, 1978.

Bennett, H. S. *Chaucer and the Fifteenth Century*. Oxford: Clarendon-Oxford UP, 1947.

Blake, Norman. *The Textual Tradition of the Canterbury Tales*. London: Arnold, 1985.

Brunot, Ferdinand. *Histoire de la langue francaise*. 1900–10. Paris: Colin, 1966. 5 vols.

Chambers, R. W., and Marjorie Daunt. *Book of London English*. Oxford: Clarendon-Oxford UP, 1931.

Christianson, C. Paul. "Evidence for the Study of London's Late Medieval Manuscript Book Trade," Griffiths and Pearsall 87–108.

Cooper, Robert L. *Language Spread: Studies in Diffusion and Social Change*. Bloomington: Indiana UP, 1982.

Crow, M. M., and Clair Olson. *Chaucer Life Records*. Oxford: Clarendon-Oxford UP, 1966.

Doyle, A. I. "English Books in and out of Court from Edward III to Henry VII." *English Court Culture in the Later Middle Ages*. Ed. V. J. Scattergood and I. W. Sherborne. New York: St. Martin's, 1983. 163–82.

Doyle, A. I., and Malcolm Parkes. "The Production of Copies of the *Canterbury Tales* and the *Confessio Amantis* in the Early Fifteenth Century." *Medieval Scribes, Manuscripts, and Libraries. Essays Presented to N. R. Ker*. Ed. M. Parkes and A. G. Watson. London: Scholar, 1978. 163–210.

Ebin, Lois. *John Lydgate*. New York: Twayne, 1985.

Edwards, A. S. G., and Derek Pearsall. "The Manuscripts of the Major English Poetic Texts." Griffiths and Pearsall 257–78.

Ferris, Sumner. "The Date of Chaucer's Final Annuity and of 'The Complaint to His Empty Purse.'" *Modern Philology* 65 (1967); 45–52.

Fisher, John H. "Animadversions on the Text of Chaucer, 1985." *Speculum* 63 (1988): 779–83.

———. "Chancery and the Emergence of Standard Written English in the Fifteenth Century." *Speculum* 52 (1977): 870–99.

———. "Chancery Standard and Modern Written English." *Journal of the Society of Archivists* 6 (1979): 136–44.

———. "European Chancelleries and the Rise of Standard Written Languages." *Proceedings of the Illinois Medieval Association* 3. Ed. Ruth E. Hamilton and David L. Wagner. DeKalb: Northern Illinois U, 1986. 1–34.

_____. *The Importance of Chaucer*. Carbondale: Southern Illinois UP, 1992.

_____. *John Gower*. New York: New York UP, 1964.

Fisher, John H., Malcolm Richardson, and Jane L. Fisher. *An Anthology of Chancery English*. Knoxville: U of Tennessee P, 1984,

Fortescue, John. *De Laudibus Legum Anglie*. Ed. and trans. S. B. Chrimes. Cambridge: Cambridge UP, 1947.

Green, Richard Firth. *Poets and Princepleasers*. Toronto: U of Toronto P, 1980.

Griffiths, J. J., and Derek Pearsall, eds. *Book Production and Publishing in Britain, 1375–1475*. Cambridge: Cambridge UP, 1989.

Grillo, R. D. *Dominant Languages: Language and Hierarchy in Britain and France*. Cambridge: Cambridge UP, 1989.

Gumperz, John J. *Language and Social Identity*. Cambridge: Cambridge UP, 1982.

Harriss, G. L. *Cardinal Beaufort*. Oxford: Clarendon-Oxford UP, 1988.

_____. *Henry V: The Practice of Kingship*. Oxford: Oxford UP, 1985.

Haugen, Einar. *The Ecology of Language: Essays by Einar Haugen*. Selected and introd. Anwar S. Dil. Stanford: Stanford UP, 1972.

Heller, Monica S. "Negotiations of Language Choice in Montreal." Gumperz 108–18.

Hoccleve, Thomas. *The Regement of Princes*. Vol. 3 of *Hoccleve's Works*. Ed. F. J. Furnivall. ES 72. Oxford: EETS, 1897.

Hutchinson, Harold. *Henry V: A Biography*. New York: Day, 1967.

Johnson, Paul. *The Life and Times of Edward III*. London: Wiedenfeld, 1973.

Legge, Mary Dominica. *Anglo-Norman Literature and Its Background*. Oxford: Clarendon-Oxford UP, 1963.

Lydgate, John. *Troy Book*. Ed. Henry Bergen. ES 97. Oxford: EETS, 1906.

Manly, J. M., and Edith Rickert. *The Text of the Canterbury Tales*. 8 vols. Chicago: U of Chicago P, 1940.

Matthew, Gervase. *The Court off Richard II*. London: Murray, 1968.

McFarlane, K. B. *England in The Fifteenth Century: Collected Essays*. London: Hambledon, 1981.

Merilees, Brian. "Anglo-Norman Literature." *Dictionary of the Middle Ages*. Vol. 1. New York: Scribners, 1982.

Misra, Bal Govind. "Language Spread in a Multilingual Setting: The Spread of Hindi as a Case Study." *Language Spread: Studies in Diffusion and Social Change*. Ed. Robert L. Cooper. Bloomington: Indiana UP, 1982. 148–57.

Mitchell, Jerome. *Thomas Hoccleve*. Urbana: U of Illinois P, 1968.

Nicholls, Jonathan. *The Matter of Courtesy*. Cambridge: Brewer, 1985.

Norton-Smith, John. *John Lydgate: Poems*. Oxford: Clarendon-Oxford UP, 1960.

Pearsall, Derek. *John Lydgate*. Charlottesville: U of Virginia P, 1970.

Pollock, Frederick, and Frederic William Maitland. *The History of English Law*. 2nd ed. 2 vols. Cambridge: Cambridge UP, 1968.

Richards, Mary P. "Elements of Written Standard in the Old English Laws." *Standardizing English: Essays in the History of Language Change in Honor of John Hurt Fisher*. Ed. Joseph B. Trahern, Jr. Knoxville: U of Tennessee P, 1989. 1–22.

Richardson, Malcolm. "Henry V, the English Chancery, and Chancery English." *Speculum* 55 (1990): 726–50.

Riley, H. T., ed. *Memorials of London and London Life*. London: Longman, 1868.

Root, R.K. "Publication before Printing." *PMLA* 28 (1913): 417–31.

Roskell, J. S. "Thomas Chaucer of Ewelme." *Parliaments and Politics in Late Medieval England*. London: Hambledon, 1983. 151–92.

Ruud, Martin B. *Thomas Chaucer*. U of Minnesota Studies in Lang. and Lit. 9. Minneapolis: U of Minnesota, 1926.

Samuels, M. L. "Some Applications of Middle English Dialectology." *Historical Linguistics*. Ed. Roger Lass. New York: Holt, 1969. 404–18.

Scanlon, Larry. "The King's Two Voices: Narrative and Power in Hoccleve's *Regement of Princes*." *Literary Practice and Social Change in Britain, 1380–1530*. Ed. Lee Patterson. Berkeley: U of California P, 1990. 216–47.

Schirmer, Walter. *John Lydgate*. Trans. Ann E. Keep. Berkeley: U of California P, 1961.

Scogan, Henry. *Moral Balade*. *The Complete Works of Geoffrey Chaucer*. Ed. W. W. Skeat. Vol. 7. Oxford: Clarendon-Oxford UP, 1894. xli. 7 vols.

Seward, Desmond. *Henry V Warlord*. London: Sidgwick, 1987.

Spurgeon, Caroline F. *Five Hundred Years of Chaucer Criticism and Allusion*. 3 vols. 1908–17. New York: Russell, 1960.

Stubbs, William. *The Constitutional History of England*. 3 vols. Oxford: Clarendon-Oxford UP, 1874–78.

Towle, George M. *The History of Henry V*. New York: Appleton, 1866.

Vale, Juliet. *Edward III and Chivalry*. Cambridge: Brewer, 1982.

Wardhaugh, Ronald. *Languages in Competition: Dominance, Diversity, and Decline*. Oxford: Blackwell, 1987.

Windeatt, Barry, ed. *Troilus and Criseyde*. By Geoffrey Chaucer. London: Longman, 1984.

Wolff, Philippe. *Western Languages*. Trans. F. Partridge. London: Wiedenfeld, 1971.

Wylie, James Hamilton. *History of England under Henry the Fourth*. 2 vols. 1884. New York: AMS, 1969.

Wylie, James H., and W. T. Waugh. *The Reign of Henry V*. 3 vols. 1914–29. New York: Greenwood, 1968.

Chronology

ca. 1343	Chaucer is born.
1357	Is recorded as a page in the household of Elizabeth de Burgh, Countess of Ulster.
1359	Lionel of Antwerp joins the King's army; Chaucer goes with him to France and is captured at Reims.
1360	March: Chaucer is ransomed for £16. October: Peace with France; Chaucer serves as emissary for Lionel between Calais and England.
1362	English replaces French as England's national language.
1366	Chaucer marries Philippa Roet.
1366	Travels to Spain; father, John Chaucer, dies; mother, Agnes Copton, remarries.
1367	June 20: Receives a pension of £20 per annum from King Edward III. Is described as a *valettus* (later a squire) in the household of the Countess of Ulster. Son Thomas is born; first session of Parliament to be held in English.
1368	Goes on a diplomatic mission to France for the King.
1368–1372	Translates part of the French *Roman de la rose* as *The Romaunt of the Rose*; produced many lyrics, including

	"The Complaint unto Pity" and "The Complaint to Our Lady".
1369	Accompanies John of Gaunt's military expedition to France. The Black Death reoccurs; the Queen dies; Blanche, Duchess of Lancaster, the first wife of John of Gaunt, dies; Chaucer writes *The Book of the Duchess*.
1370	Goes to France again, on a governmental or military mission with John of Gaunt.
1371	John of Gaunt marries his second wife, Constance of Castile.
1372	Goes to Genoa and Florence, Italy, for diplomatic reasons; Philippa Chaucer serves in the household of John of Gaunt's wife.
1372–1377	Writes poems that later become "The Monk's Tale" and "The Second Nun's Tale".
1374	Receives a pension from John of Gaunt; he receives a daily pitcher of wine for life from the King; he is granted a house over Aldgate; he becomes Controller of the Customs in London.
1375	Becomes the guardian of two boys.
1376–1378	The Black Prince dies; Chaucer travels repeatedly to Europe to pursue marriage negotiations for Richard; King Edward III dies and is succeeded by Richard II, Edward's grandson.
1378	Richard II doubles the annuity given to Chaucer by Edward III.
ca. 1380	Writes *Saint Cecelia* and *Anelida and Arcite* and *Palamon and Arcite*.
1380	Is accused of rape; the victim acquits him. Son Lewis is born.
1381	The Peasants' Revolt; writes *The House of Fame*; Chaucer's mother dies.
1384	Writes *The Parliament of Fowls*.

1385	Writes *Troilus and Criseyde*; is granted a permanent deputy in Customs.
1386	Gives up the house over Aldgate and ends his job as Controller of the Customs and serves as Justice of the Peace in Kent (until 1389). Becomes Member of Parliament in Kent. Writes *The Legend of Good Women*.
1387	Begins *The Canterbury Tales*. His wife Philippa dies.
ca. 1389	Writes *Sphere*.
1389–1390	July 12: Is appointed Clerk of the King's Works at Westminster; supervises the building of scaffolds for tournaments and the repair and construction of other buildings. Becomes Commissioner of Walls and Ditches.
1391	Withdraws from his Works office and, in June, becomes Deputy Forester of the Royal Forest in Somerset.
1391–1392	Writes the bulk of *The Treatise of the Astrolabe*.
1393	The King grants Chaucer £10 for his work.
1394	Death of Constance, second wife of John of Gaunt; death of Queen Anne; Richard II grants another annuity of £20 for life.
1396	John of Gaunt marries his mistress, Katherine Swynford, widowed sister of Chaucer's wife.
1399	John of Gaunt dies. King Richard II is deposed, and Henry IV, son of John of Gaunt, becomes king.
1400	Richard II is murdered; Chaucer dies.

Works by Geoffrey Chaucer

All dates are necessarily approximate.

The Book of the Duchess, 1369
The House of Fame, 1381
The Parliament of Fowls, 1384
Troilus and Criseyde, 1385
The Legend of Good Women, 1386
The Canterbury Tales, begun 1387
Sphere, 1389
Treatise on the Astrolabe, 1391–1392, with later additions

Works about Geoffrey Chaucer

Boitani, Pierre and Jill Mann, eds. *The Cambridge Chaucer Companion.* Cambridge: Cambridge University Press, 1986.

Crow, Martin M., and Clair C. Olson, eds. *Chaucer Life-Records.* Oxford: Clarendon Press, 1966.

Dillon, Janette. *Geoffrey Chaucer.* New York: Palgrave, 1993.

Gardner, John. *The Life and Times of Chaucer.* New York: Knopf, 1977.

Hanwalt, Barbara A. *Chaucer's England.* Minneapolis: University of Minnesota Press, 1992.

Lerer, Seth. *Chaucer and His Readers.* Princeton: Princeton University Press, 1996.

Miller, Robert P., ed. *Chaucer: Sources and Background.* New York: Oxford University Press, 1977.

Morse, Ruth. *Chaucer Traditions.* Cambridge: Cambridge University Press, 1990.

Patterson, Lee. *Chaucer and the Subject of History.* Minneapolis: University of Minnesota, 1991.

Rossignol, Rosalyn. *Chaucer A–Z.* New York: Facts on File, 1999.

Rowland, Beryl, ed. *A Companion to Chaucer Studies.* 2nd ed. New York: Oxford University Press, 1979.

Rudd, Gillian. *The Complete Critical Guide to Geoffrey Chaucer.* The Complete Critical Guides to English Literature. London and New York: Routledge, 2001.

Singman, Jeffrey L. *Daily Life in Chaucer's England.* New York: Greenwood, 1995.

Weever, Jacqueline de. *A Chaucer Name Dictionary: A Dictionary of Astrological, Biblical, Historical, Literary, and Mythological Names.* New York: Garland, 1986.

West, Richard. *Chaucer: 1340–1400: The Life and Times of the First English Poet.* New York: Caroll & Graf, 2000.

Wilkins, Nigel. *Music in the Age of Chaucer.* New York: Boydell & Brewer, 2000.

WEBSITES

The New Chaucer Society
ncs.rutgers.edu/

Chaucer MetaPage
www.unc.edu/depts/chaucer/

A Brief Chronology of Chaucer's Life and Times
icg.fas.harvard.edu/~chaucer/special/varia/life_of_Ch/chrono.html

Island of Freedom: Geoffrey Chaucer
www.island-of-freedom.com/CHAUCER.HTM

The Canterbury Tales Project
www.shef.ac.uk/uni/projects/ctp/index.html

The Online Medieval and Classical Library
sunsite.berkeley.edu/OMACL/

The Internet Medieval Sourcebook
www.fordham.edu/halsall/sbook.html

The Labyrinth: Resources for Medieval Studies
http://www.georgetown.edu/labyrinth/labyrinth-home.html

Contributors

HAROLD BLOOM is Sterling Professor of the Humanities at Yale University and Henry W. and Albert A. Berg Professor of English at the New York University Graduate School. He is the author of over 20 books, including *Shelly's Mythmaking* (1959), *The Visionary Company* (1961), *Blake's Apocalypse* (1963), *Yeats* (1970), *A Map of Misreading* (1975), *Kabbalah and Criticism* (1975), *Agon: Toward a Theory of Revisionism* (1982), *The American Religion* (1992), *The Western Canon* (1994), and *Omens of Millennium: The Gnosis of Angels, Dreams, and Resurrection* (1996). *The Anxiety of Influence* (1973) sets forth Professor Bloom's provocative theory of the literary relationships between the great writers and their predecessors. His most recent books include *Shakespeare: The Invention of the Human*, a 1998 National Book Award finalist, and *How to Read and Why*, which was published in 2000. In 1999, Professor Bloom received the prestigious American Academy of Arts and Letters Gold Medal for Criticism.

ELLYN SANNA has authored more than 50 books, including adult non-fiction, novels, and young-adult biographies. She works as a freelance editor and manages the editorial service Scriveners' Ink.

BONITA M. COX is an Assistant Professor of English at San José State University. She holds a Ph.D. from Stanford University.

GEORGE LYMAN KITTREDGE formerly of Harvard University, was a noted authority on the English language, Shakespeare, and Chaucer in the early part of the 20th century.

LARRY D. BENSON earned a Ph.D. from the University of California at Berkeley and is currently the Francis Lee Higginson Research Professor at Harvard University. His work in the field of medieval literature has been extensive, and he has served as the editor of *The Riverside Chaucer* and *The Canterbury Tales: Complete* (2000).

JOHN H. FISHER, is a Professor Emeritus of English at the University of Tennessee.

INDEX